MODERN LEGAL STUDIES

LAW REFORM
AND
THE LAW COMMISSION

AUSTRALIA
The Law Book Company Ltd.
Sydney : Melbourne : Brisbane

CANADA AND U.S.A.
The Carswell Company Ltd.
Agincourt, Ontario

INDIA
N. M. Tripathi Private Ltd.
Bombay

ISRAEL
Steimatzky's Agency Ltd.
Jerusalem : Tel Aviv : Haifa

MALAYSIA : SINGAPORE : BRUNEI
Malayan Law Journal (Pte.) Ltd.
Singapore

NEW ZEALAND
Sweet & Maxwell (N.Z.) Ltd.
Wellington

PAKISTAN
Pakistan Law House
Karachi

MODERN LEGAL STUDIES

LAW REFORM
AND
THE LAW COMMISSION

by

JOHN H. FARRAR, LL.M.

Lecturer in Law at the University of Bristol

SWEET & MAXWELL
1974

Published in 1974 by
Sweet & Maxwell Limited of
11 New Fetter Lane, London
and printed in Great Britain
by Northumberland Press Limited
Gateshead, Co. Durham

SBN Hardback   421 17790
       Paperback   421 17800

CONTENTS

OTHER BOOKS IN THE SERIES:

GENERAL PREFACE TO MODERN LEGAL STUDIES

Modern Legal Studies is a series written for students of law in Universities, Polytechnics, and other institutions of higher education. It originated in the belief that law students need a series of short, scholarly monographs in different areas of the law, resembling those now being produced in other fields of social science.

The Series has five principal aims. First, it aims to supplement traditional textbooks by providing opportunity both for new topics to be written about and introduced into the syllabus of traditional courses, and for older topics to be given deeper consideration than they receive in the standard texts. Secondly, as the series progresses, it aims to provide a possible alternative to the one-textbook-per-course approach of many law courses; a set of several short books in, for instance Property Law, could be used as substitutes for the present all-purpose texts. This would enable the student to become acquainted with a variety of views and approaches to the subject. Thirdly, the existence of a series of small, relatively cheap, legal monographs will, it is hoped, facilitate the breaking of boundaries between traditional courses—*e.g.* Contract and Tort,—and the creation of new courses built upon monographs in the Series.

Fourthly, the Series aims to promote greater consideration on the part of other social scientists of the legal aspects of social political and economic problems who are too often discouraged from considering the law on a whole range of matters because of the daunting nature of legal textbooks. Without compromising on the standards of legal scholarship, a smaller monograph should prove less formidable and therefore more useable. Fifthly, and by no means least in importance, the Series offers an outlet to legal scholars in the United Kingdom and elsewhere. The Editorial Board hopes that, where they have something worth saying to a wider audience than their own students, but which does not fit the length of either a law review article or a full-length book, they will be stimulated to prepare a monograph for the Series.

Modern Legal Studies then has ambitious aims, which will be realised only with time. But it is very much a co-operative venture, between the authors, who have written or are writing for the Series, the Editorial Board, and the wider community of legal scholars, teachers and students who are both the consumers now and, it is hoped, the producers of the future.

J. P. W. B. McAuslan
University of Warwick

PREFACE AND POLEMIC

In the Founders' Memorial Lecture which she delivered at Girton College in 1956 entitled "Law as it looks to a Historian" Helen Cam concluded "The form and the spirit of law may differ widely from age to age and from nation to nation. But with all its crudities, its clinging to obsolete techniques, its lapses from human decency and indorsements of inhumanity, law stands out in history as one of the noblest expressions of the human struggle to solve the problem— how to make life good." The greater the population grows, the more urbanised society becomes and the more sophisticated and complex it is, the more crudity, obsolescence and inhumanity in the law become apparent and, in an open society, criticised. There develops a need to keep the law up to date with the changing facts and *mores* of society— a need in short for law reform and law reform bodies.

It is one of the more conjectural theses of this book that the Law Commission set up in 1965 was set up too late in the day. The law had not developed to keep pace with a rapidly changing society in a number of areas, in its techniques and in the basic system of litigation, which all needed a thorough overhaul by the 1930's. Various governments nibbled at the problem—the Law Revision Committee and other part time bodies were set up. Legal aid was introduced. If anything legal aid tended to exacerbate the problem, as reports like Beeching showed. It is the writer's view that the Law Commission is the biggest and best advance that has been made in law reform machinery in England but that by itself or together with the surviving part time bodies and the occasional *ad hoc* royal commission and departmental committee it is not enough to keep pace even with national law reform let alone Common Market harmonisation and approximation and other international projects.

Because this is arguably the case the English Legal System depends more than ever before upon the work and active involvement of academic lawyers to write "doctrine," initiate creative reform ideas, serve on or with reform bodies and measure the social effectiveness of law reform. They must seize this opportunity which Continental and American Academics have seized before them in their own countries. They must no longer be content with the inferior and impotent role into which as a group they have been cast by some of the more blinkered of their practising brethren. A large number of practical instances does not *per se* constitute a universe nor give the person experiencing them omniscience. However, before academics educate and reform society they must educate and reform themselves so that individually and collectively they render the most positive contribution to law reform. This means in practical terms that they must be prepared to spend time, learn more about legislative drafting, assimilate more ideas from foreign systems and literature in germane disciplines, co-operate with social scientists and re-organise their rather ineffective law reform committees in the Society of Public Teachers of Law for instance into smaller working groups capable and willing to do *ad hoc* projects for the Law Commission. Perhaps the new Institute of Advanced Legal Studies building could be used as a base for these activities. Such work is, and ought to be regarded as, equally if not more important than the production of another gratuitous thesis, article or text book.

So much by way of polemic. It has been difficult in writing this book to trap such a dynamic subject into a satisfactory text. The text itself was basically written up to the end of July, 1973. Since that time the Law Commission's Eighth Annual Report has been published and a summary of its main provisions are given in a postscript contained in Appendix F.

At a very late stage in the printing and following the General Election the resignation of the Heath Government took place and the incoming Prime Minister, Harold Wilson, announced the appointment of Sir Elwyn Jones as Lord Chancellor on March 5, 1974. It is to be expected that as a contributor to 'Law Reform Now' he will show something of the enthusiasm for law reform demonstrated by its editor, Lord Gardiner, during his Chancellorship.

Although I have made a number of references to the Scottish Law Commission this book is primarily about Law Reform and the English Law Commission. I have enough knowledge of Scots Law to realise that I am not competent to deal with Law Reform and the Law Commissions. This, rather than a narrow Chauvinism on my part, is the reason for the title and the emphasis in the text.

I would like to thank a number of my friends who have assisted me during the authorship of this book. In particular (but without prejudice to the generality of the foregoing) I would like to thank David Williams for a great deal of help with Chapter 8 and Dirk Meure, Tony Dugdale and David Yates for particular points and general criticisms. I am also grateful to members of the Law Commission and to the secretaries of various law reform bodies at home and abroad for their assistance in my research. My main regret is that the confines of space have limited my use of the material. Finally, I would like to thank Patrick McAuslan, the general editor of this series, for his comments and encouragement and Rosemary Wiltshire and Margaret Edwards for making sense of the hieroglyphics of my manuscript.

JOHN FARRAR
University of Bristol

TABLE OF CASES

TABLE OF STATUTES

CHAPTER 1

THE CONCEPT OF LAW REFORM AND THE EVOLUTION OF LAW REFORM INSTITUTIONS

LAW reform is a familiar and important concept and yet one which has about it a certain basic ambiguity. In one sense many instances of law-making in a legal system by the courts or the legislature can be regarded as law reform. There is usually some pre-existent law which the courts or Parliament amend or replace. To that extent there is reform inherent in the law-making function. If there is no pre-existent law on a particular topic then it is arguable that one cannot logically have law reform.

However, just as a critic once observed of the War Office that they were always busy in preparing for a previous war, the views of the judiciary are, in Dicey's words, apt to correspond to the opinions of the day before yesterday. Judicial innovation is also necessarily piecemeal.

Law reform has, therefore, over the last 150 years acquired a more specialised meaning to cover the situation where the inherent tendency of the courts to develop the law is accelerated by increased legislative intervention. Law reform in this sense comprehends reform of the substance and the form of the law and the institutions of the legal system. The improvement of legal education is also closely connected with law reform although it is not usually regarded as part of it. Nevertheless, it is commonly thought that the better educated a lawyer is, the greater his appreciation of the strengths and weaknesses of the rules and institutions of the system in which he later practises will tend to be. Of course this does not necessarily follow and conclusive empirical evidence is absent. Perhaps, however, this is "common sense."

Sometimes law reform is subdivided into two categories, one usually described as "lawyers' law reform" and the other by a variety of names such as "political" or "administrators' law reform" or "social-economic reform." To be more precise perhaps the categories should be described as reform of "lawyers' law" and reform of "politicians' or administrators' or social and economic law."[1]

By the first category is meant case law and legislation which over the centuries has been developed almost exclusively by lawyers and which is regarded as too technical for laymen to handle. By the second is meant the ever expanding body of law giving expression to political, economic and social reforms. This latter category is generally defined so widely that it is impossible to separate it from the first category at least in theory, although it has sometimes for reasons largely of convenience been separated in practice. The dichotomy is unfortunate, however, since it can lead to the view that "lawyers' law" is without social context and importance which is an obvious fallacy.

In the words of Pound, law must be stable and yet it cannot stand still.[2] The principal forces in society which activate change vary from time to time in nature and effect but in modern society there are government and the political parties; public opinion stimulated by the mass media; pressure groups of differing size and influence; the permanent officials in the government departments; the more forward looking members of the practising and academic legal professions and lastly the official law reform bodies. Ranged against these are forces which have also varied. In 1952 Professor Goodhart[3] identified them mainly as particular attitudes of mind shared by lawyers and laymen alike; natural conservatism and fear of change; the claim that a particular change is contrary to the spirit and traditions of the law; lack of knowledge of what can be done and then, lastly, lack of adequate machinery.

This book is about the institutions and methods of law reform. The aim of the remainder of this chapter will be to trace, albeit in the barest detail, an outline of the evolution of the institutions of law reform in the United Kingdom up to the creation of the Law Commissions in 1965.

In the early history of the common law, the Crown, as the fountain of justice, was not only the source of law, it was also the source of law reform in the first sense. Justice emanated from the King in Council. Gradually the common law courts separated from the Council and achieved some measure of law reform mainly by the means of equity in the Aristotelean sense and fictions, but this power, together with their basic power of adjudication, was derived from the Crown. For some considerable period the Chancellor and later the Court of Chancery exercising the extraordinary jurisdiction of the Crown performed a useful law reform function in fact if not in theory. Parliament was in its nascent stage and it was not until the seventeenth century that it was regarded as a possible law reform agency. Until then, in the words of Sir Matthew Hale, changes were accomplished by wise men, not rashly or hastily but upon "due and weighty advice and consideration."[4]

However, by the beginning of the seventeenth century some of the wise men had become complacent. To Coke the common law was the perfection and the embodiment of reason—"the golden metwand whereby all men's causes are justly and evenly measured."[5] There were, however, notable dissentients and it was here that we first see law reform assume a distinctly political aspect. Coke's eulogy of the common law was in a sense cunningly disguised self-praise and justification. By his manipulation of authorities and by means of fictions the common law was judicial law-making in opposition to Stuart absolutism. This was perceived by James I and Bacon who in turn favoured reform of the common law. Bacon made a number of criticisms of the common law; it was uncertain; the laws were so many that it was not possible for the common people to put them into practice or even for lawyers to understand them fully. The "heaping up of laws without digesting them maketh but a chaos and confusion and turneth the laws many times to become but snares for the people."[6] The solution, Bacon thought,[7] lay in a restatement in the form of digests of case law and statute laws. Obsolete and overruled cases should be omitted, contradictory laws reconciled and judges should have the power to give authoritative rulings on points of law without litigation. When new legislation was prepared earlier enactments on the same subject should be repealed and an entirely new law substituted. Bacon did not, however, favour codification—"I dare not advise to cast the law into a new mould. The work which I propound tendeth to pruning and grafting the law and not to ploughing up and planting it again; for such a remove I should hold indeed for a perilous innovation."[8] In order to keep the law up to date six commissioners should be appointed to investigate obsolete and contradictory laws and to report to Parliament regularly so that appropriate legislation could be introduced. The appointment of the commissioners should be reviewed every three or five years. In these proposals we see the seeds of ideas which were to be repeated in John Austin's lectures and which perhaps led eventually to the creation of the Law Commissions in 1965.

Bacon had the King's enthusiastic support. Indeed, James went even further and favoured codification. Mr. Veale, in his learned work, *The Popular Movement for Law Reform 1640-1660* sees (probably rightly) in these proposals an attempt to restore to the Crown supreme law-making power. Be that as it may, the proposals came to nothing. Nevertheless, within the next thirty years the history of law reform took a paradoxical turn. Law reform changed from being the property of absolute monarchists and became the ambition of the republicans. In the interregnum, Cromwell was sympathetic to the cause of law reform and set up a commission headed by Matthew Hale. Pamphlets abounded during this period advocating all manner of reforms of the courts, procedure and substantive law. The cause of law reform was taken up (*inter alia*) by the distinguished lawyer, William Sheppard, who in *England's Balme* advocated codification. At one stage, in a sublime moment, the Parliament of Saints contemplated replacing the whole of the laws of England by the Ten Commandments. The great schemes, however, resulted in little practical reform. The vested interests opposing reform were too powerful.

Thereafter, the little reform which occurred was for over a century and a half largely the result of judicial law-making. Even here the ingenuity of a judge of the calibre and distinction of Lord Mansfield was fettered by his more pedestrian colleagues on the Bench. *Quieta non movere* was the order of the day in law as well as politics. The common law lapsed again into a mood of complacency and self-congratulation so well expressed in Blackstone's elegant prose.

The nineteenth century, however, saw drastic changes in the legal system largely resulting from the influence of the Utilitarians, in particular, Bentham. "The age of law reform and the age of Jeremy Bentham are one and the same" said Lord Brougham.[9] "He is the father of the most important of all the branches of reform, the leading and ruling department of human improvement. No-one before him had ever seriously thought of exposing the defects in our English system of jurisprudence. All former students had confined themselves to learn its principles—to make themselves masters of its eminently technical and artificial rules; and all former writers had but expounded the doctrines handed down from age to age.... He it was who first made the mighty step of trying the whole provisions of our jurisprudence by the test of expediency, fearlessly examining how far each part was connected with the rest; and with a yet more undaunted courage, inquiring how far even its more consistent and symmetrical arrangements were framed according to the principle which should pervade a code of laws—their adaptation to the circumstances of society, to the wants of men, and to the promotion of human happiness." These were the words of a reforming Chancellor of the period and in the view of Dicey "strike the right note."

Subscribing wholeheartedly to the *a priori* principles of utility, Bentham sought to remodel the laws of England in accordance with them. These were his premises, which he applied with rigorous logic; legislation was his method; codification was his aim. Bentham's eccentric life as a semi-recluse working unceasingly for his cause has been portrayed by Hazlitt, Romilly and John Stuart Mill. Why did his work gain acceptance? Maine, writing in 1861,[10] thought that the secret of Bentham's immense influence was the fact that he gave English lawyers a clear rule of reform which hitherto they had lacked. Dicey shared this view and added that many of the reformers were not actual utilitarians but were all, consciously or unconsciously, profoundly influenced by utilitarian ideas. "They were men of the world ... they loved practical compromises as much as Bentham loved logical deductions from strict principles."[11] As the liberalism of the nineteenth century, it was the utilitarianism not of the study but of the House of Commons and the Stock Exchange. Indeed, Bentham's appeal extended to the ranks of the Peelites amongst the Conservatives. The reason in Dicey's view was that " 'legislative' utilitarianism is nothing else than systematised individualism, and individualism has always found its natural home in England."[12]

Reform in earnest started after Brougham's famous six-hour speech indicting English law and the legal system in the House of Commons in 1828. Thereafter, numerous commissions were set up.[13] The pattern in the first half of the nineteenth century was generally to have commissions consisting exclusively of lawyers and John Austin called for a complete reconstruction by a law commission of "scientific lawyers." The Benthamite influence led initially to law reforms promoting the rights of the individual and a gradual rationalisation of the court structure. Dicey, tracing law and opinion in the nineteenth century, discerned a second trend which followed this, that of collectivism which shifted the attention of law reform from the individual to the group and from the middle class to the working class. Reforms which took place marked the abandonment by the legislature of *laissez-faire* principles in the interests of workers, the public and the state and included the repeal of the Combination Acts, the improvement of working conditions and the introduction of compulsory insurance against industrial injuries.[14] In the growth of collectivism and the increasing paternalistic role of the state, it is noticeable that the institutional pattern of law reform began to change. Commissions were not appointed solely from lawyers, although lawyers were often members of them. Also, the departments of state such as the Board of Trade and the Home Office played an increasing role in reform of the law falling within their province and provided the continuity which had always been lacking in reform by royal commission. Bentham, Lord Langdale and Lord Westbury called for a Ministry of Justice but their cries had gone unheard. It was only during the Chancellorship of Lord Selborne that the Lord Chancellor's office was built up.[15]

In 1918, Lord Haldane's Committee on the Machinery of Government[16] called for a Minister of Justice to exercise the functions of the Home Secretary and Lord Chancellor in connection with legal administration with "experts charged with the duty of watching over the necessities of law reform, and of studying the development of the subject at home and abroad." The Committee's proposals were strongly supported by the Law Society and opposed by the Bar Council for rather hysterical reasons.[17] The idea was dropped.

Throughout the nineteenth century, there were movements in the legal profession in favour of codification. Bentham's original aim had gone further than earlier schemes and had been a codified law of England, replacing the common law; the abolition of judicial law-making and an annual review of the code. Professional opinion fluctuated considerably in the nineteenth century but there were few who agreed with the whole of Bentham's scheme.

In India there were successful experiments in codifying areas of the common law[18] and it was felt by many that such success could be achieved at home. Lord Westbury, ever conscious of what he described as "our inferiority in jurisprudence," had raised the matter in Parliament in 1863 recalling Bacon's project in the seventeenth century and in 1866 a royal commission was set up under Lord Hanworth "to enquire into the expediency of a Digest of Law."[19] The commission recommended the adoption of digests of particular branches of the law and jurists were invited to submit their work. In 1876, Sir James Fitzjames Stephen, former draftsman of some of the Indian codes, published his Digest of the Law of Evidence, followed in 1877 by his Digest of the Criminal Law. The latter was nearly enacted but was eventually dropped. In 1877, Sir Frederick Pollock published his Digest of the Law of Partnership. Later, in bill form, after a decade of parliamentary machinations and alterations and deletions almost amounting to mutilations, this reached the statute book as the Partnership Act 1890. Judge Chalmers' Digests of the Law of Bills of Exchange and Sale were respectively reduced to bill form and enacted as the Bills of Exchange Act 1882 and the Sales of Goods Act 1893. The attitudes of Pollock and Chalmers to their work were modest; their achievements great. To Pollock codes were not meant "to dispense lawyers from being learned, but for the ease of lay people and the greater usefulness of law."[20]

Parliament, having enacted much legislation, aimed at reforming the law and the legal system turned its attention more to social policy and reform of "politicians' law" in the early part of the twentieth century. The legal profession, having exhausted much of its zeal in the reforms of the nineteenth century, were by and large content to lapse into another of its periods of complacency and self-congratulation, particularly with regard to the Judicature Acts, which for some time remained the topic of judicial eulogy. The failure during this period to attempt a comprehensive simplification and reform of substantive law was unfortunate as we shall see.

Initiative was, however, taken by Lord Birkenhead in the 1920's, piloting through Parliament the legislation of which Lord Haldane had been the architect and which produced the long needed codification of the reforms in the law of real property which had been taking place in the previous century. The 1925 legislation also reduced the number of legal estates and provided for vesting of settled land in the tenant for life and for registration of encumbrances.

In 1934, Lord Sankey, Lord Chancellor in the National Government and a keen law reformer, set up the Law Revision Committee with membership drawn from the judiciary and the practising and academic legal professions. Its mandate was "to consider how far, having regard to the Statute Law and judicial decisions, such legal maxims and doctrines as the Lord Chancellor may from time to time refer to the Committee require revision in modern conditions ..." The setting up of this Committee was described by Viscount Kilmuir L.C. in 1957 as "the source of the modern machinery of law reform."[21] The original initiative had in fact been taken by a Liberal Member of Parliament, Mr. Llewellyn-Jones, in 1932, who moved a resolution in the House of Commons on the need for law reform, which was passed unanimously. The charges which had been levelled against the legal system of the time were first that, while the bulk of the law was rational, there were still numerous defects and anomalies, secondly, the unsystematic shape of the law and the need for more consolidation and codification; and thirdly, numerous defects in procedure. Following the debate Donald Somervell, then a young Conservative M.P. and later law officer then judge, wrote a memorandum to Sir Claud Schuster, Permanent Secretary to the Lord Chancellor, suggesting the setting up of a committee. Sankey and Schuster had been thinking on these lines and after some discussions the Committee was set up. The reason for the delay was that Lord Hanworth, its first chairman, was occupied with another Committee on the Business of the Courts.[22]

The Committee sat until 1939.[23] Its terms of reference left the initiative to the Lord Chancellor of the day. Thus, while Viscount Sankey was a keen reformer and remitted seven important questions to the Committee in its first year, Viscount Hailsham who succeeded him was less keen, and only referred two questions in three years. Initially, it consisted of fourteen lawyers—Lord Hanworth, Master of the Rolls, as chairman, together with four other judges, four practising barristers, two members of the Law Society, Sir Claud Schuster and two academic lawyers. Later, when Lord Wright replaced Lord Hanworth as chairman, the number of academic lawyers increased to five.

The Committee prepared eight interim reports initially working with great speed to produce four reports on more specific points, later taking longer on more general questions. The reports were comparatively brief; the Committee relying on the knowledge and experience of its members and Professor Gutteridge's learning in comparative law. There was a high degree of unanimity in the reports and all but one of its reports were implemented in a series of Law Reform Acts in the period 1934 to 1935. The exception was the sixth report on the Statute of Frauds and the doctrine of consideration. Details of the reports and the resulting legislation are given in Appendix A at the end of this book.

With the outbreak of war, the work of the Committee fell into abeyance, although it was never formally dissolved.

During the post-war years, there was no possibility of devoting parliamentary time to what Viscount Kilmuir described as the "reform of pure lawyers' law." Kilmuir, addressing the annual conference of the Society of Public Teachers of Law in Belfast in 1957, said "I think Lord Chancellors of whatever political complexion have always taken the view, which I certainly share, that it is not right to entrust committees with the onerous task of considering and recommending reforms if there is no reasonable assurance that parliamentary time can be found for giving effect to the resulting recommendations, for the precious time of eminent men serving as members of committees should not be wasted."[24]

There were, however, a number of *ad hoc* committees and royal commissions set up to consider particular problems which reported between 1945 and 1952, in particular, Lord Porter's Committee on the Law of Defamation, Lord Morton's Committee on Intestate Succession and Lord Tucker's Committee on Limitation of Actions. Their recommendations were implemented in legislation in the period 1952 to 1954.

Nevertheless, the need was felt for the revival of a standing committee on law reform. The Society of Public Teachers of Law sent a deputation to Lord Jowitt in 1950, calling for this. Jowitt was sympathetic but his hands were tied by the pressure of the post-war Socialist legislation. He did, however, reconstitute the Statute Law Committee to perform the technical role of keeping the statute book up to date by consolidation and statute law revision. The Law Revision Committee under the new name of the Law Reform Committee was formally constituted in 1952 by his Conservative successor, Lord Simonds.

Its terms of reference were "to consider, having regard especially to judicial decisions, what changes are desirable in such legal doctrines as the Lord Chancellor may from time to time refer to the Committee." Professor Wade pointed out in an article in the *Modern Law Review* in

1961[25] that these were more restrictive than those given to the previous Committee (which included statute law). This seems to be overstating the case a little since the terms merely directed the Committee to pay special attention to precedent. In practice, as Professor Wade himself admits, there has been little difference in the type of subject considered.

The Law Revision Committee had its critics and Lord Simonds took the opportunity to cure some of the defects. Thus, the new Committee was expressly empowered to work through sub-committees and frequently makes use of this power. It was given power to co-opt. It was given a permanent secretariat consisting of members of the Lord Chancellor's office. Lord Kilmuir, in his address to the S.P.T.L., said this latter factor had proved useful in that it promoted direct liaison between the Lord Chancellor and the Committee and gave the Lord Chancellor's staff the necessary background knowledge when the time comes for consultations with other departments and briefing of parliamentary counsel on legislation to implement a report.

Lord Justice Jenkins was appointed chairman and three members of the old Committee were reappointed. The usual membership has been five judges, five practising barristers, two solicitors and three academic lawyers. Pursuant to its powers the new Committee appointed small sub-committees presided over by a judge to which academic lawyers expert in the particular field were co-opted. These prepared preliminary drafts which were finally settled by the whole Committee. This is a technique which in some respects has been followed by the English Law Commission.

The Committee still exists under the chairmanship of Lord Justice Orr and has produced nineteen reports of which twelve have been implemented in legislation. The present membership comprises six judges, three professors, two Queen's Counsel and two solicitors. Again particulars of the reports and the resulting legislation appear at the end of this book, in Appendix B.

The main criticisms[26] which have been levied at the Law Reform Committee are that the initiative and choice of topics remains with the Lord Chancellor of the day and depends on his enthusiasm for law reform. This criticism, however, is more apparent than real since in practice the Committee has from time to time submitted possible subjects to the Lord Chancellor for remission to themselves.

Secondly, the Committee tends to be composed of lawyers and the need was felt for lay representation. A similar point, as we shall see, was made at the time of the creation of the Law Commissions but was of no avail. Meanwhile, on *ad hoc* commissions lay representation has increased and it is particularly noteworthy that the Royal Commission on Quarter Sessions and Assizes was chaired by a layman, Lord Beeching. Coupled with the criticism of lack of lay representation was the criticism that the Committee did not always receive evidence and make known sufficiently to the public the problems it was investigating.

Thirdly, the Committee suffers through being a part-time body. Lord Gardiner, in a speech in the House of Lords, described how work on the Committee "meant attending about one afternoon a quarter after a long day's work for about one and a half hours." In his words they were given "a little tiny piece of law to look at and after about two years produced ... very useful reports."

A major criticism voiced by academic lawyers has been the Committee's neglect of foreign and Commonwealth law. Being a part-time body it obviously lacked research facilities but it did not always make the best use of what facilities were available in the universities.

Lastly, a frequent criticism which has been made not so much of the Committee as of parliamentary procedures generally is that there is not adequate machinery in Parliament for introducing and expediting law reform proposals.

Such matters have tended to depend on the fortuities of private members' bills.[27] We shall return to these criticisms in more detail in later chapters, when we consider the extent to which the creation of the Law Commission has answered them.

The Private International Law Committee was set up in 1952 by the Lord Chancellor, a year after the drafting of a charter designed to place the Hague Conference on a lasting footing by the establishment of a permanent bureau. The Committee published five reports and last reported in 1963. Although it has never been technically wound up, it now appears to be moribund.

The Criminal Law Revision Committee was set up in 1959 by R. A. Butler as Home Secretary as "a standing committee to examine such aspects of the Criminal Law of England and Wales" as the Home Secretary might refer to it "to consider whether the law requires revision and to make recommendations." The Committee continues in existence under the chairmanship of Lord Justice Edmund Davies and half its membership consists of judges while the remainder includes three distinguished academics and the Director of Public Prosecutions. At the time of writing the Committee has produced twelve reports of which nine have been implemented. Particulars appear in Appendix C. Where legislation is necessary the practice has been adopted of annexing a draft Bill to the report, a practice which as we shall see has been adopted by the Law Commission. As regards legislative enactment of the proposals there has sometimes been differences of detail between the Act and the draft Bill but with the exception of section 16 of the Theft Act 1968 (which was not proposed by the Committee and which is currently under review by them) there does not appear to have been differences of substance.

The working methods and procedures of the Committee are necessarily affected by the nature of its membership which is exclusively part time. On average the full Committee holds ten to twelve meetings a year, each lasting a whole day. Frequency of meetings, however, is affected by factors such as the number of references made to it at any one time and whether a sub-committee has been set up.

As regards consultation, the nature and extent depend upon the subject under review. On two of the most recent references on Evidence and on Offences against the Person, before starting work the Committee wrote to a large number of persons and bodies concerned with the administration or teaching of law asking for their views on the matters included in the terms of reference. In addition the chairman consulted a great many of the judiciary. On the Evidence reference the Committee again consulted these persons and bodies setting out the substance of the recommendations which they were considering making and asked for comments on them. Individuals with specialist knowledge which is particularly relevant to an aspect of the law under consideration may be invited to serve as co-opted members on a sub-committee or on the full Committee or to attend a meeting of the Committee. Thus on the Evidence reference the Committee had the help of seven representatives of the police when identification evidence and police investigations were being considered. Lastly, each time a subject is referred to the Committee this is announced in Parliament and the press and the public are invited to send their observations to the Committee.

A Law Reform Committee for Scotland was set up by the Lord Advocate in 1954 consisting of the judiciary, practitioners and academics. This was later to lapse on the setting up of the Scottish Law Commission.

As regards non-governmental agencies the Law Society and the General Council of the Bar now have their own specialist committees which take an active interest in law reform. Political associations of lawyers such as the Haldane Society, the Inns of Court Conservative Association and the Society of Labour Lawyers all take an interest in law reform.

Justice, the British branch of the International Commission of Jurists, represents a cross section of lawyers, academics and laymen interested in the Rule of Law and Human Rights and produces reports which are often influential.[28] And, lastly, of course, specialist organisations and pressure groups take initiative in relation to matters of reform of interest to themselves. The role of the latter in the formation of public opinion and the impetus to law reform are matters to which we shall return in Chapter 6.

Notes

[1] See E. C. S. Wade "The Machinery of Law Reform" in (1961) 24 M.L.R. 3, 4-5. See the interesting remarks of Lord Devlin and Sir Leslie Scarman in a BBC discussion published in *What's wrong with the Law?*, pp. 86-87. See also Geoffrey Sawer, *Law in Society*, pp. 126 *et seq*. He uses the term "law of administration."

[2] *New Paths of the Law*, p. 1, 13.

[3] Law Reform—address to the Holdsworth Club, pp. 9 *et seq*.

[4] "Considerations touching the Amendment of Laws" published in F. Hargrave, *Law Tracts* (1787), Vol. 1, pp. 249-89. Benjamin Cardozo wrote of this period "The artifice was clumsy, but the clumsiness was in some measure atoned for by the skill of the artificer" —"A Ministry of Justice" (1921) 35 H.L.R. 113.

[5] 4th Institute, p. 240.

[6] See Veale, *The Popular Movement for Law Reform 1640-60*, p. 70.

[7] See *Advancement of Learning*, Book VIII, Chapter III.

[8] Veale, *ibid*., p. 70.

[9] *Speeches* (1838), Vol. II, p. 287.

[10] *Ancient Law*, pp. 78, 79.

[11] *Op. cit*., p. 169.

[12] *Ibid*., p. 175.

[13] See F. E. Dowrick "Lawyers' Values for Law Reform" in (1963) 79 L.Q.R. 556.

[14] See generally Sir William Holdsworth, *A History of English Law*, Vols. XIV and XV.

[15] See the history in Lord Birkenhead's *Points of View*, Vol. 1, pp. 92 *et seq*.

[16] Report of the Committee on the Machinery of Government, Cmd. 9230 (1918).

[17] See Abel-Smith and Stevens, *Lawyers and the Courts*, pp. 131-32. See the more cogent reasons of Lord Birkenhead, *op. cit*.

[18] See *The Anglo-Indian Codes* (ed. Whitley Stokes), Vol. I—General Introduction—and Pollock's Introduction to *A Digest of the Law of Partnership* (1887), p. x.

[19] See generally J. H. Baker, *An Introduction to English Legal History*, p. 299.

[20] *Digest of the Law of Partnership* (1915 ed.), p. viii.

[21] (1957) 4 J.S.P.T.L. (NS) 75.

[22] Kilmuir, *ibid.*, at p. 80.

[23] See Dowrick, *op. cit.*, pp. 568 *et seq.*

[24] *Op. cit.*, p. 81.

[25] (1961) 24 M.L.R. 3.

[26] See Wade, *op. cit.*; Dowrick, *op. cit.*, pp. 577 *et seq.* and W. T. Wells Q.C., M.P., "The Law Commission; an interim appraisal" in (1966) 37 *Political Quarterly* 291, 292.

[27] For the experiences of one seasoned promoter of private members' legislation, see Leo Abse, *Private Member* (1973.

[28] As for instance, its report on "The Ombudsman" which influenced the passing of the Parliamentary Commissioner Act 1967.

Chapter 2

THE CLIMATE OF IDEAS PRIOR TO 1965

WE have seen how the pattern of law reform changed from *ad hoc* commissions to more permanently established but part-time bodies. There were gradual improvements in the system. The Lord Chancellor's department increased in personnel. Nevertheless, the need was felt for a drastic reappraisal of the system. The call for reform of the institutions of reform was not just limited to left-wing politicians, although it is amongst radical lawyers that consistent enthusiasm was maintained.

In 1933, in a Fabian pamphlet,[1] a committee of the Haldane Club reiterated the arguments for the establishment of a Ministry of Justice. They argued that there was nobody specifically responsible for law reform which was, of course, then true. Fundamental reorganisation was necessary. The position of the Lord Chancellor was peculiar. He was not reponsible to the House of Commons. It was necessary to have a Minister of Justice in the House of Commons to exercise supervision over law reform, legal education and the drafting of legislation. He should absorb some of the functions of the Home Secretary, Lord Chancellor and Attorney-General. The aim would be unity and co-ordination. The call was repeated in 1951 by the Haldane Society in the collection of essays entitled "The Reform of the Law."[2] It was suggested[3] that the Lord Chancellor's office should be broken up and that there should be two or more Commissioners of the Great Seal over whom the Lord Chancellor might exercise supervisory powers. One of these should always be a member of the House of Commons and have responsibility for law reform. He would be a Minister of Justice in effect, if not in name.

A variation of this theme was put forward by Mr. Harvey Moore Q.C. in a letter to *The Times*[4] in 1952. He suggested that a Minister should be created called the Vice-Chancellor who should be responsible to the Lord Chancellor for law reform. Lord Schuster, on the other hand, in a letter to *The Times*[5] a few days later suggested a third law officer, the Queen's Advocate, should be appointed to assist the Lord Chancellor in matters of law reform.

Professor Goodhart, in his Holdsworth Lecture in 1952,[6] favoured the appointment of a new permanent official in the Lord Chancellor's office to deal with law reform.

Even less ambitious was the view expressed by Professor C. J. Hamson in a broadcast talk later published in "Law Reform and Lawmaking[7]: A Reprint of a Series of Broadcast Talks" in 1953. What was required in his view above all was a developing and expanding common law under the leadership of the judges who were willing "to re-assume a responsibility ... primarily theirs—namely again to enunciate, in a form adequate and appropriate to our times, the fundamental principles of the judge made part of our law."

In the first edition of his book *The Machinery of Justice* which had been published in 1940 Professor R. M. Jackson had regarded a Ministry of Justice as desirable in the interests of law reform but by the third edition in 1960 he attached less importance to it. While not unduly dismayed by the arrangements for reform of substantive law he was inclined to attribute lack of progress in reform of procedure and the structure and organisation of the courts to the complacency of lawyers as a class. "The peculiarity of the legal system is its blind devotion to its shortcomings." For this, he appeared to suggest, the remedy lay in a reformed system of training of the legal profession.

In an article in the *Law Quarterly Review*[8] in 1953, Gerald Gardiner Q.C., having considered the various proposals, came down against the idea of a Ministry of Justice and favoured leaving the responsibility for law reform in the main with the Lord Chancellor, assisted by a Minister in the House of Commons to be called the Vice-Chancellor. The Vice-Chancellor should be a lawyer and be responsible to the Lord Chancellor. In addition, the Vice-Chancellor should have a permanent secretary and sufficient staff. Thus, at this time, Gerald Gardiner's views were very much a synthesis of the middle of the road reformist views.

In a Fabian pamphlet entitled "Speed-up Law Reform"[9] (1958) Robert Pollard supported the appointment of a Vice-Chancellor to sit in the House of Commons. He also suggested that the Lord Chancellor should appoint a Law Reform Council of lawyers and laymen to advise on the progress of law reform; that the Speaker of the House of Commons should be given power to certify any Bills as non-contentious; that there should be provision of special facilities for the passage of the Bills through Parliament; and lastly that a commission of full-time experts should be set up to codify the law of England.

In the Preface to his book *Samples of Lawmaking*[10] published in 1962, Lord Devlin, after expressing scepticism on judicial law-making in the modern age and discussing the inadequacies of the part-time law reform committees concluded "I believe that it would be beneficial if there were a small body of men who devoted the whole of their time, writing perhaps with the aid of a lawyer body of consultants meeting from time to time, to a systematic tidying up of the law as well as to making proposals for wider reforms." He prophesied that statutes prepared in this way would be the most prolific source of law reform in the future.

In 1963 Gerald Gardiner was joint editor with Dr. Andrew Martin of a collection of esays entitled "Law Reform Now."[11] In Chapter 1, which was to become the blueprint for the Law Commissions, his views had grown more radical. Gardiner and Martin argued that it was difficult to think of a rational argument against reorganising the Lord Chancellor's office as a Ministry of Justice. The argument based on tradition was purely emotional and the argument that the independence of the judiciary was undermined in countries which had a Ministry of Justice was illfounded.

Nevertheless, the editors were disinclined to press for a change of name but rather to press the case for strengthening and reorganising the Lord Chancellor's office which should include a strong unit concerned exclusively with law reform in a wide sense including codification. The head of the unit should carry the rank of Minister of State and be called Vice-Chancellor and he should sit in the House of Commons. As we shall see this latter suggestion was not implemented.

The Vice-Chancellor should preside over a committee of not less than five highly qualified lawyers who were to be described as Law Commissioners and whose office would be created by statute. Their appointments would be full-time for periods not less than three years. Remuneration should be left to the Lord Chancellor to agree with Treasury consent. The Law Commissioners should not be ordinary civil servants but should enjoy a high degree of independence. Their chief responsibility would be to review, bring up to date and keep up to date the general law which was defined as "the common law and equity, and also that part of the statute law which does not fall within the province of any particular government department." The Law Commissioners should not necessarily be excluded from dealing with what was described as "administrators' law." They should always be consulted and should not be debarred from taking initiative where no initiative was forthcoming from the department primarily responsible.

The Law Commissioners were to draw up a long term plan for the systematic review of the general law and to

consider proposals for reform. To assist them they should
have a staff of legal assistants and parliamentary draftsmen.

There would then be no need to maintain the Law Reform
Committee, the Private International Law Committee and the
Home Secretary's Criminal Law Revision Committee as
permanent institutions. They could, however, be re-
established *ad hoc* for any major project the Law Commissioners might refer to them. The Government's powers to
appoint royal commissions and other *ad hoc* committees
should continue but should only be exercised in consultation
with the Law Commissioners.[12]

It is rumoured that early implementation of the "Law
Reform Now" proposals was made a condition of Gerald
Gardiner's acceptance of the Lord Chancellorship in the
Wilson Government.[13] Whilst this cannot be confirmed
Gerald Gardiner did become Lord Chancellor and most of
the proposals were adopted in the White Paper of 1965 and
implemented in the Law Commissions Act 1965.

Notes

[1] "A Ministry of Justice"—New Fabian Research Pamphlet No. 6,
1933. In his book *In Quest of Justice* published in 1931, Claud
Mullins had pinned his hopes on a Lord Chancellor relieved of his
judicial duties and obligations as Speaker of the House of Lords.

[2] "The Reform of the Law," edited by Glanville Williams. See
also Herber Hart, *The Way to Justice*, Chapter 9, for similar views.

[3] *Ibid.*, p. 14.

[4] *The Times*, March 18, 1952.

[5] *The Times*, March 24, 1952.

[6] "Law Reform" (1952) published by the Holdsworth Club of the
University of Birmingham.

[7] "The Machinery of Law Reform in England" (1953) 69 L.Q.R.
46, 61-62.

[8] (1953) 69 L.Q.R. 46, 57 *et seq.*

[9] "Speed-Up Law Reform", Fabian Research Series No. 194.

[10] p. 27.

[11] "Law Reform Now" ed. by Gerald Gardiner and Andrew
Martin.

[12] *Ibid.*, at pp. 7 *et seq.*

[13] See "The Law Commissions Act 1965" by Lord Chorley and
G. Dworkin in (1965) 28 M.L.R. 675, 679.

CHAPTER 3

THE CREATION OF THE LAW COMMISSIONS

THE Law Commissions Bill was introduced into the House of Commons and given its First Reading on January 20, 1965. The Second Reading took place on February 8 and the Bill received the Royal Assent on June 15. The speedy passage of the Bill was directed by the Lord Chancellor in the House of Lords and Sir Eric Fletcher, Minister without Portfolio, in the House of Commons.[1] To digress slightly, Sir Eric, now Lord Fletcher, was a solicitor who in this respect acted as a "Vice-Chancellor" in the House of Commons. His appointment as Minister with Portfolio with these responsibilities was to a large extent experimental. The immediate objective was to set up the Law Commissions but it was also contemplated that he would be responsible in the House of Commons for piloting through the measures of law reform which emanated from the Law Commissions. Lord Fletcher states that there was inevitably a time lag before this became feasible. He was also expected to and did assist the law officers and various government departments notably the Treasury in connection with legislation passing the House of Commons where the assistance of a quasi-law officer was needed and where for various reasons neither the Attorney-General or the Solicitor General was available. Lord Fletcher has informed the writer that there were objections to setting up the office of Vice-Chancellor and that in his view it was not constitutionally satisfactory to have a Minister without Portfolio with ill-defined functions. Lord Fletcher considers that once the Law Commissions were operating there was no strong case for setting up in government the office of Vice-Chancellor or Minister of Justice. We shall, however, return to this topic later.

The Law Commissions Bill was accompanied by a White Paper setting out the Government's policy.[2] The aim was to modernise, to simplify and to consolidate. This was the theme of Sir Eric Fletcher's speech, moving the Second Reading of the Bill in the House of Commons.[3] The Government rejected the proposal to create a Ministry of Justice.[4] It had never had widespread support in the country and there had been changes in the structure and functions of the Lord Chancellor's office which made it better fitted to discharge its increasing administrative functions. What was needed was adequate machinery to cope with law reform.

The major reaction of the opposition was predictable—scepticism at the need for a new body and concern at the expense. In the words of Sir John Hobson,[5] the Bill was "merely an elaborate piece of expensive machinery designed to perform functions for which there is already full Ministerial responsibility. It adds an unnecessary spare wheel to the present machinery which is quite capable of meeting the necessity for accelerating law reform." The main problem was the delays caused by parliamentary procedures.

The Conservatives were, however, divided. Some amongst their number were enthusiastically in favour of the idea.[6]

Sir Eric Fletcher conceded that there was a difficulty with parliamentary procedures but did not put forward plans for overcoming it.[7]

In the House of Lords the Bill received broadly based support, including strong support from a maiden speech by Lord Wilberforce[8] who argued that non-lawyers ought to be involved in the Law Commissions' business—law reform was "much too serious a matter to be entrusted to lawyers." This latter suggestion was not taken up by the Government in the Act but has been taken up in practice by the Law

Commissions by means of sub-committees and widespread consultation.

Reference was also made to the problems of parliamentary time and lack of parliamentary draftsmen. Viscount Simonds made the caustic point[9] that the cost of the Law Commissions would provide an incentive to Parliament to allot time for the implementation of their proposals. Lord Morris of Borth-y-Gest[10] made a more constructive point by suggesting that the Standing Committee of the House of Lords on Bills dealing with law, courts and procedure which had sat from 1889-1891 might be re-convened. However, it was felt that the problem arose not so much in the House of Lords as the House of Commons.

The other important item of a general nature which arose during the course of the debate was a reference in the House of Lords' debate to an article by the legal correspondent of *The Guardian* which "leaked" the names of the first commissioners. An attack was made by the opposition on the left wing bias of the proposed appointments—an attack that Lord Gardiner did not altogether answer.[11] In the words of the late Lord Tangley (a former President of the Law Society sitting as a cross-bencher) "the verdict of the profession would be that one would have a High Court judge, a practising barrister and three Leftish dons"[12]—a situation which later took place but not with the catastrophic consequences envisaged by his lordship.

The Bill was amended in minor particulars[13] and became the Law Commissions Act 1965.

Notes

[1] See generally "The Law Commissions Act 1965" by Lord Chorley and G. Dworkin in (1965) 28 M.L.R. 675.

[2] Cmnd. 2513.

[3] H.C. Deb., Vol. 706, cols. 47 *et seq*.

[4] *Ibid.*, col. 52.

[5] *Ibid.*, col. 60.

[6] See *e.g.* Daniel Awdry at col. 73, Sir Hugh Lucas-Tooth at cols. 96 *et seq.*

[7] *Ibid.*, col. 54.

[8] H.L. Deb., Vol. 264, cols. 1171 *et seq.*

[9] *Ibid.*, col. 1189.

[10] *Ibid.*, col. 1215.

[11] See further Chorley and Dworkin in (1965) 28 M.L.R. at p. 684.

[12] H.L. Deb., Vol. 265, col. 452.

[13] For a discussion of the amendments see Chorley and Dworkin, *op. cit.*, pp. 683 *et seq.*

CHAPTER 4

THE LEGAL POWERS AND PRACTICE OF THE LAW COMMISSIONS

Legal powers

The opening sections of the Law Commissions Act[1] created two law commissions, one to be known as the Law Commission—which was for England and Wales—and another to be known as the Scottish Law Commission, for Scotland.

It was felt that the great differences between the two systems in areas such as property and criminal administration justified separate commissions.[2] It was intended that the two commissions should, however, work together in close cooperation. Indeed, to a certain extent they were placed under a statutory obligation to do so by section 3(4) which provided that they should "act in consultation with each other." However, although it is nowhere written into the Act, Sir Eric Fletcher said that he imagined that the English Law Commission would assume final responsibility.[3] In respect of what and to whom was not made clear.

Both commissions were to consist of a chairman and four other commissioners. The English Law Commissioners were to be chosen from persons "appearing to the Lord Chancellor to be suitably qualified by the holding of judicial office or by experience as a barrister or solicitor or as a teacher of law in a university."[4] In other words, all lawyers. Scottish Law Commissioners were to be chosen by the Secretary of State for Scotland and the Lord Advocate from persons of similar categories.[5]

It is interesting to note here that the Act did not limit the qualifications to those obtained in the United Kingdom. In his speech on the Second Reading of the Bill in the House of Commons, Sir Eric Fletcher said[6] that although this would normally be so in the case of barristers and solicitors, an academic lawyer might well have gained most or some of his experience outside the United Kingdom, in the Commonwealth or possibly in the United States.

The Law Commissioners were to be appointed for a term not exceeding five years subject to reappointment.[7] A judge could be appointed Law Commissioner and retain his office as judge in the meantime.[8] Sir Eric Fletcher commented[9] that just as experience as a judge would be of value to a Commissioner, so would service on the Commission prove useful to a judge on his return to the bench. The experience of the Law Reform Committee had proved the value of what he called "cross-fertilisation" in this field.

The remuneration of persons other than judges was to be subject to negotiation between the Lord Chancellor or the Secretary of State and the Commissioners subject to approval of the Treasury.[10]

The Act also provided[11] for additional staff to be appointed by the Lord Chancellor or the Secretary of State. The expenses of the Law Commissions were to be defrayed out of funds provided by Parliament.[12]

Section 3 of the Act defined the duties and powers of the Law Commissions.[13] First it was their basic duty to take and keep the law under review with a view to its systematic development and reform, including in particular codification, the elimination of anomalies, the repeal of obsolete enactments, consolidation and generally the simplification and modernisation of the law. It is to be noted that although the act contemplated codification it did not in fact require it.[14] To execute their basic duty they were authorised to consider proposals for reform, to submit to the appropriate Minister (*i.e.* for England and Wales, the Lord Chancellor) programmes of law reform, and then, when approval had been given, to undertake the examination of particular items in the programme and to formulate proposals for reform by means of draft Bills or otherwise.

Where the programme covered a branch of the law which seemed likely to be controversial in a political sense or to have a broad social trend it was unlikely that the detailed review would be entrusted to the Commissioners themselves. In cases like that it was thought by the Government that it would be more appropriate that the matter should be referred in accordance with the usual practice to a royal commission or a departmental committee.[15]

The Commissioners were further authorised to prepare (at the request of the Minister), comprehensive programmes of consolidation and statute law revision and to undertake the preparation of draft Bills, to give advice and information to government departments and other bodies at the instance of the government, together with proposals for reform of any branch of law and lastly, the Commissioners were authorised and instructed to obtain such information on other legal systems as appeared to them likely to facilitate the performance of any of their functions.[16]

The Act set out certain procedures with regard to Law Commission business. Section 3(2) provided that the Minister should lay before Parliament any programmes prepared by the Law Commission and approved by him and any proposals for reform formulated by the Commission pursuant to the programmes. Each Commission should make an annual report to the Minister of their proceedings and the Minister should lay the report before parliament with such comments (if any) as he thought fit (s. 3(3)).

The general effect of these provisions was described by Sir Leslie Scarman in his Manitoba Law School Foundation Annual Lecture in 1967.[17] By the Act, he said, the law of England and Scotland shifted its emphasis from reliance on judicial law-making to reliance on legislation to reform the law. It meant that Parliament has accepted "a greater, continuing responsibility for reform of the law than in our history it has ever accepted before." However, "Parliament, in matters of law reform, is an extremely amateur and indolent body. It requires advice and it requires spurring on and to be stimulated into action." The Act was, therefore, an attempt to provide Parliament with the advice which it needs in order to reach a skilled decision and to provoke it to action.

Personnel

The first English Law Commissioners were, as *The Guardian*'s legal correspondent had forecasted, Sir Leslie Scarman (Chairman), Professor L. C. B. Gower, Mr. Neil Lawson Q.C., Mr. N. S. Marsh and Professor Andrew Martin Q.C.[18] All of them were appointed as full time Commissioners. Sir Leslie Scarman was a distinguished judge of the High Court who was to show creative genius in his new and unprecedented role; Professor Gower had at one time been a partner in a London firm of solicitors and was an eminent academic lawyer while Mr. Lawson was a leading counsel at the Commercial Bar before retiring shortly before his appointment as a Law Commissioner. Mr. Marsh was a former Oxford law don who had been Director of the British Institute of International and Comparative Law since 1960 after serving as Secretary-General of the International Commission of Jurists. Professor Martin was in practice at the Bar and was Professor of International and Comparative Law at Southampton University. He was also co-editor of "Law Reform Now."

A major criticism levelled at these appointments was that they did not include a full-time practising solicitor. This was later met at least in part by the appointment of Mr. A. S. Cotton, a member of the Council of the Law Society, as "special consultant." In the words of Lord Chorley and Professor Dworkin he was to be "a part-time sixth Commissioner."

The first Scottish Commissioners were Lord Kilbrandon, a judge of the Court of Session as Chairman, Mr. G. D. Fairburn, Writer to the Signet, Professor J. M. Halliday of Glasgow University and Professor T. B. Smith Q.C., of Edinburgh University.

The English Law Commission was given modest premises at Conquest House, John Street, near Gray's Inn, which it shares with an Inspector of Taxes, and set to work to recruit a small staff of lawyers from government departments, the professions and academic life. Parliamentary draftsmen were seconded to them. At the time of the First Annual Report 1965-66, the total staff numbered thirty-five. This consisted of the secretary, four draftsmen, nine other lawyers and twenty-one non-legal members of staff. The policy was to remain small but to recruit able and enthusiastic lawyers, especially young ones. Also, the rhythm of work was necessarily uneven, so a larger staff might result in waste of manpower as well as institutional introspection.[19]

It was stated in the Second Annual Report that the policy of recruiting young lawyers for temporary appointments before entry into government service, practice or academic life had been successful.[20]

In the period 1969-72 there was a change of personnel. Professor Andrew Martin retired and was replaced by Mr. Claud Bicknell, a solicitor in private practice who had been a partner in a firm in Newcastle upon Tyne since 1939. Mr. A. S. Cotton retired in 1970 as special consultant, although he continued as part-time consultant on land law. Mr. Neil Lawson Q.C. was appointed a High Court judge on April 19, 1971, and his place was taken by Mr. Derek Hodgson Q.C., of the Northern Circuit. Mr. Hodgson was a former judge of the Salford Hundred Court of Record, a Recorder and member of the Ormrod Committee on Legal Education. Professor

Gower was appointed Vice-Chancellor of Southampton University on October 1, 1971, and was succeeded by Professor Aubrey Diamond of Queen Mary College, London, well known for his work on the law relating to the consumer and his membership of various consumer protection bodies. In December 1972 Sir Leslie Scarman retired on his appointment to the Court of Appeal and was replaced by Sir Samuel Cooke who had been a High Court judge of the Queen's Bench Division since 1967 and of the National Industrial Relations Court since 1972. He combines with his judicial experience a distinguished academic background, service as Assistant then Parliamentary Counsel to the Treasury, practice at the Bar and membership of the Senate of the Four Inns of Court. At the time of the Seventh Annual Report the full-time staff numbered fifty-one consisting of the secretary, four draftsmen, nineteen other lawyers and twenty-seven non-legal staff. In addition, the Commission was assisted by Parliamentary Counsel, including Sir Noel Hutton Q.C., formerly First Parliamentary Counsel, who undertook the drafting of the code of landlord and tenant law. There were also several other outside lawyers who rendered assistance on a part-time basis. In the Seventh Annual Report the Law Commission state that they intend to rely on this kind of assistance more in future and a small number of academic lawyers have begun to do part-time work. It would appear that more use could be made of the latter.

By contrast the Scottish Law Commission works with less resources. At the beginning only the chairman had a full-time appointment. Later in 1968 Mr. A. M. Johnston Q.C., Sheriff of Dumfries and co-editor of Gloag and Henderson's *Introduction to the Law of Scotland*, replaced Mr. Fairburn as Commissioner but was given a full-time appointment. Professor A. E. Anton of Glasgow was appointed as a part-time member. On September 30, 1971 Lord Kilbrandon ceased to be chairman on his appointment as a Lord of

Appeal in Ordinary and Mr. Johnson ceased to be Commissioner on his appointment as a Senator of the College of Justice as Lord Dunpark. Lord Hunter, Senator of the College of Justice, replaced Lord Kilbrandon and Mr. Ewan Stewart Q.C., former Solicitor-General for Scotland replaced Mr. Halliday as full-time Commissioner. Professor T. B. Smith became a full-time member in 1972 and Professor Anton a full-time member in 1973. In the beginning the staff consisted of a secretary, assistant secretary and three other lawyers. Later, however, Sir John Gibson Q.C. joined them on his retirement from the office of Legal Secretary to the Lord Advocate to assist with drafting work where he worked with an advocate and solicitor. The Commission has always been located in the Old College of Edinburgh University where it can use the library facilities.

One refreshing note is that the Scots have employed four senior law students in their summer vacation as well as using working parties and *ad hoc* researchers and consultants.

Practice

The English Law Commission took the view from the outset that it would be inexpedient to lay down hard and fast rules of procedure.[21] It was felt better to adjust their working methods to the particular requirements of each individual project.

However, certain basic working methods were evolved. The Commission's usual practice was not to ask for evidence but to prepare working papers which they then circulated "to pave the way for informed consultations."[22] The internal working procedure[23] leading to the working paper is as follows. Each item in the programme is allocated to a team headed by one or more of the Commissioners. Each team is generally the master of its own procedure. The first task of the team is to prepare a working plan, that is, a phased programme of research and consultations. The working plan is then submitted to the Commissioners for comment and approval. Once approved, the plan is put into operation and the team make periodic progress reports to the Commissioners. Ultimately a working paper is produced setting out the existing state of the law and often referring to the position under other jurisdictions. It indicates defects which the Commissioners consider to exist and their provisional proposals for reform.

The working papers are then distributed to such organisations and individuals as they think it desirable to consult. These include lay organisations as well as lawyers. Copies are sent to the press and television broadcasting services. They are also on sale at Her Majesty's Stationery Office. In their Seventh Annual Report the Law Commission recognised that this method is not necessarily sufficient in itself and in the case of Family Property they introduced into the consultative phase a new feature—the publication of a statistical survey conducted at their request by the Social Survey Division of the Office of Population Censuses and Surveys into the attitudes and actions of married persons in respect of their property (see diagram). In the light of this experience the Law Commission hopes to evolve a standard procedure for harnessing the social sciences to law reform which will become as much a part of their method as the working paper procedure itself. It remains to be seen whether this is anything other than a laudable but somewhat nebulous statement of intent.

Once the working paper has been reconsidered in the light of consultations it is then produced as a report and where legislation is proposed, with draft clauses appended. Even then the Commission's responsibility does not cease. In their Fifth Annual Report[24] the Law Commission mentioned that the practice had developed whereby those responsible for the report continued to assist Parliament at various stages of the Bill by being on call if consultation were needed on

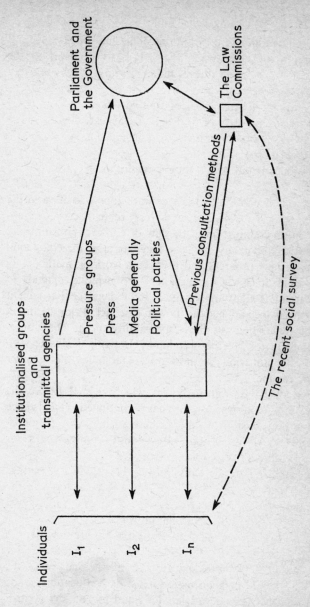

Individuals

Institutionalised groups
and
transmittal agencies

I_1

I_2

I_n

Pressure groups

Press

Media generally

Political parties

Parliament and
the Government

The Law
Commissions

Previous consultation methods

The recent social survey

LAW REFORM—the traditional and the emerging patterns of
consultation.

possible amendments or additions. This has usually been at the committee stages when the details as opposed to the general policy of the Bill are under scrutiny. It was felt that the existence of such help ensured that piecemeal amendments did not destroy the cohesion of the draft Bills and further ensured clarity of drafting. It was felt, however, that the Law Commission's assistance would be needed on a more formal basis for the codification Bills when they were produced and that thought ought to be given to the matter.

Liaison between the two law commissions was close in the early period. Thus in the first year there was active co-operation on codification of the law of contract and informal consultations on many subjects. Regular joint meetings took place to review progress and to discuss working methods.

The English Law Commission's responsibility extends to such part of the law of Northern Ireland as the Parliament of Northern Ireland had no power to enact. Prior to direct rule the remainder was the responsibility of the Director of Law Reform for Northern Ireland. He worked closely with the Law Commission but now no longer holds office under the new regime.

The English law reform bodies which existed before the Law Commission was set up have continued in existence although the division of labours between the Law Commission and the Criminal Law Revision Committee was for some time ill-defined.

The English Law Commission has held regular meetings with the General Council of the Bar, the Law Society and the Society of Public Teachers of Law. It has also participated in seminars organised at various universities.

The Law Commission laid its First Programme before Parliament on October 27, 1965. This represented a mammoth and perhaps unrealistically optimistic and ambitious work load including such major items as codification of the law of contract, crime and landlord and tenant and controversial legal topics such as contracting out of common law liabilities. Since then a Second Programme was laid before Parliament in 1968 and a Third Programme in 1973. The latter is concerned with private international law and sets up a joint working party of the English and Scottish Law Commissions to consider draft conventions emanating from the European Communities Commission's Working Group on Private International Law and the Hague Conference.

A programme in respect of consolidation and statute law revision was laid before Parliament on January 26, 1966. A further programme was laid before Parliament in 1971.

From time to time the Law Commission has given advice on law reform matters to the other government departments, although one is left with the impression that at times it has been looked upon as an intruder by some civil servants. The Department of Trade and Industry has, for instance, jealously guarded its traditional areas of responsibility with the result that there has been little reform of company law until the recent proposals and no reform of bankruptcy law. The apparent lack of consultation on the effects of joining the Common Market seems, to say the least, frightening and is perhaps an augury of things to come. However, it does seem that more recently both law commissions have been involved in some of the work of harmonisation and approximation of legislation emanating from Unidroit, the Council of Europe and the European Commission. We shall return to this subject in Chapter 8.

A list of the Law Commission's programmes and reports and the legislative enactment of its proposals appears in Appendix E.

Returning to Scotland,[25] the Scottish Law Commission has basically worked in similar ways to the English Commission but until recently it has been handicapped by the fact that a majority of its members were part-time. In the same way as the English Commission the first and second programmes were perhaps over ambitious and unrealistic. Nevertheless one perceives a strong note of realism which appears to permeate the whole of the general remarks of the Scottish Commission's Seventh Report.[26] They have taken stock, looked at their experience at home and in co-operation with the Law Commission and learned some valuable lessons which they now appear to be teaching the Law Commission.

The first lesson is that the work of formulating proposals for the reform of a large area of law is bound to be extremely time consuming and cannot be hurried without serious disadvantage. Bearing this in mind the Scottish Law Commission reconsidered how they could use their limited resources to the best advantage and came to two main conclusions. First, they thought that they should concentrate more on the large subjects in their law reform programmes and on the provision of advice to government departments and others under section 3(1)(e) of the Law Commission Act 1965. Secondly, they thought they should plan carefully in advance the resources which should be devoted to each large subject in their programmes and the order in which particular areas should be considered. In the light of the latter they decided that lower priority would have to be given to informal requests for advice as work on such requests had in the past involved interruption and delay in their programme subjects which were of greater long term importance. The activities of the Law Commission with its larger resources and of European and other international bodies dealing with reform and harmonisation of law made heavy demands on the resources of the Scottish Law Commission in reacting to them. These demands would increase with our entry into the Common Market.

The Scottish Law Commission went on to consider in detail the strength and weaknesses of their relationship with the English Law Commission. They considered that their small resources worked to their disadvantage in two situations; first, where they were jointly examining the same large area of law and secondly, where the Law Commission were considering a large area of law which was not in the Scottish Law Commission's programmes. In the former situation their main difficulty was to keep pace. The latter, however, gave them more anxiety and they openly confessed that they were receiving papers on the codification of English criminal law which contained implications of some importance to the criminal law of Scotland and to which they were unable to allocate a Commissioner or a member of the legal staff to give specific consideration.

Another disadvantage was that on a number of occasions in the year under review they had been forced to work to a tight time table. Concentration on these matters resulted in neglect of other important matters.

They made some telling criticisms of the methods adopted on codification. They found it wasteful to embark on codification of any area of law before the difficulties in that area had been identified and corrected and the necessary decisions reached on questions of principle. One would have thought that this was almost axiomatic but it often requires a stroke of genius to state the obvious. They also thought that careful consideration should be given to the form and style of codification which should be adopted in any particular field of law. The Scottish Law Commission said: "We venture to suggest that Parliamentary draftsmen in future may sometimes be called upon to alter radically their style of presentation where the subject matter is considered appropriate for codification."[27] We shall return to this later in Chapters 5, 7 and 9.

The Commission then turned to consider the difficult question of harmonisation. They recognised that there would be stronger pressures to harmonise the laws of Scotland and England, not only with one another, but also with European systems. They believed that this was sensible in certain areas of law provided that "Scots law is permitted to make its distinctive and valuable contribution." They viewed with disfavour ill-considered attempts to unify the laws of England

and Scotland by the application of principles which were alien to Scots law. They mentioned the Crowther Report on Consumer Credit as an example containing a number of instances of this fault. It also occurred during the preliminaries of the preparation of some United Kingdom legislation when inadequate consideration was given to Scots law.

Professor D. M. Walker writing on the Seventh Report in the *Scottish Law Times* of May 4, 1973[28] said that the report records a good deal of disappointment and frustration and not very much progress. He thought that the problems which the Scots Law Commission faced coping with English, United Kingdom and European materials was paralleled also at the level of practising and academic lawyers who frequently could not find the time to react to and comment on the proposals made by the Scottish Law Commission. He considered that the process of "reacting" was of some importance particularly if the "reaction" should be unfavourable. He made some caustic remarks about attempts to bring Scots law "into line" with English law. Usually he thought that this stemmed from English insularity and ignorance, the belief that because it is English it must be right. He said "it would be a good thing sometimes to bring English law into line with Ruritanian law."[29] It is by no means clear quite what he meant by the latter remark. He welcomed the spirit of independence and of disagreement with and refusal to be dragged along behind the Law Commission. He thought, however, that more progress should have been made with consolidation and ended by saying "there is certainly no danger of a Scottish code in our life-times, and Stair, Erskine and Bell will not be discarded for a long time."[30]

If Professor Walker is correct in his assumptions and he certainly seems to be justified on the basis of the comments contained in the Seventh Annual Report, it is a cause for regret that much of the harmony which the Law Commissions Act envisaged and in fact required, should have been lost. There is more than ever before a need for such co-operation.

Notes

[1] The Law Commissions Act 1965, ss. 1 and 2. On the Act and the whole of the subject-matter of this chapter see Norman Marsh Q.C.'s paper "Law Reform in the United Kingdom: A New Institutional Approach" in (1971) 13 William & Mary L.R. 263 and the articles are cited in his extremely useful Bibliography at pp. 302-03.

[2] See Sir Eric Fletcher at H.C. Deb, vol. 706, col. 55.

[3] *Ibid.*, col. 56.

[4] s. 1(2). It would seem a little unfair to limit law teachers to those who teach in universities. See also K. W. Wedderburn "Reflections on Law Reform," *The Listener*, May 6, 1965, at p. 685, for the view that one of the Law Commissioners should have been a sociologist. See further chapter 9 and the references there cited.

[5] s. 2(2).

[6] H.C. Deb., Vol. 706, col. 53.

[7] s. 1(3) and s. 2(3).

[8] s. 1(4) and s. 2(4).

[9] H.C. Deb. Vol. 706, col. 53.

[10] s. 4.

[11] s. 5.

[12] s. 4(4) and s. 5(4).

[13] s. 3(1)(*a*)–(*f*).

[14] See further Sir Leslie Scarman, "A Code of English Law?"— a lecture given to the University of Hull in 1966, p. 3.

[15] Sir Eric Fletcher at H.C. Deb., Vol. 706, col. 54-55.

[16] For discussions of the importance of the latter provision see L. Neville Brown, "Comparison, Reform and the Family," an inaugural lecture at the University of Birmingham, pp. 2-4 and Norman Marsh Q.C., "Quelques Réflexions Pratiques Sur l'usage de la Technique comparative dans la Réforme du Droit National" in (1970) 47 *Revue de Droit International et de Droit Comparé* 81.

[17] (1968) 3 Manitoba L.J. 47, 50.

[18] See further Chorley and Dworkin (1965) 28 M.L.R. at pp. 684-687.

[19] See the Law Commission's First Annual Report (Law Com. No. 4), p. 3.

[20] Second Annual Report (Law Com. No. 12), p. 3.

[21] First Annual Report, p. 3; Second Annual Report, p. 3.

[22] Second Annual Report, p. 3.

[23] First Annual Report, p. 6.

[24] Fifth Annual Report (Law Com. No. 36), p. 2.

[25] See generally D. M. Walker, "Reform, Restatement and the Law Commissions" in (1965) *Judicial Review* 245.

[26] Scot. Law Com. No. 28, pp. 2-3.

[27] *Ibid.*, p. 3.
[28] *Op. cit.*, p. 119-121.
[29] *Ibid.*, p. 120.
[30] *Ibid.*, p. 121.

CHAPTER 5

REFORM OF THE MEDIUM FOR LAW REFORM

THE Law Commissions' functions are essentially advisory. Their recommendations can only be directly effected through the medium of legislation.[1] The commissions, therefore, have a vital interest in improving the drafting, interpretation and arrangement of statute law. In this chapter we will consider first the linguistic problems involved in legislation which they have to face and then the Law Commissions' recommendations for interpretation of statutes and their work in consolidation, statute law revision and codification.

Linguistic problems

There have been in the past some philosophers who have maintained the innate incapacity of language to convey thought and our impressions of the real world accurately. Indeed, such views can be found in the writings of lawyers such as Ellesmere and Plowden in the sixteenth century[2] providing intellectual justification for the "Equity of the Statute" idea. What troubled philosophers such as Bishop Berkeley[3] (as, indeed, it had troubled Aristotle long before in his discussions of law, equity and justice[4]) was the inescapable presence in language of widespread generality and abstraction. The language we use seems abstract and thin compared with the immediacy and concreteness of living experience. In the words of Professor Max Black,[5] to some writers, "Where reality is a web of specific, particular, individual things, each with its own tang, language now appears as a disembodied ballet of abstractions."[6] Such views, though superficially convincing, when analysed closely amount to a demand that the description of a thing in words should evoke the full experience of perceiving the thing itself. This is to demand too much. The role of language is not to duplicate reality but to communicate.

Nevertheless, language sometimes fails as a means of communication. At times, the fault lies not in our words but in ourselves—through misunderstanding, lack of experience or plain ignorance. At other times, however, the fault lies in aspects of language itself. Modern idiom proliferates words and phrases which are clichés suffering from what Black aptly calls "semantic anaemia." Also a word used may have two or more meanings giving rise to a contextual ambiguity. The three main species of ambiguity are homonymy (where the same word sound has two distinct meanings), polysemy (the usual case where a word has many senses regularly attached to it) and amphiboly (uncertain grammatical construction, e.g. the definition of anthropology as "the science of man, embracing woman").[7]

In addition, some words are vague or "open textured," e.g. words such as "reasonable," "just and equitable," "fair."[8] The law makes use of such vague or loose concepts which are valuable in determining borderline cases by removing some of the arbitrariness of the classification systems which we seek to impose on the continuum of the real world in law-making. The use of such concepts legitimatises ad hoc but reasoned choice in a borderline case. It has been described as "a precisely appropriate degree of imprecision."[9]

To combat the evils of these aspects of language, the cure for semantic anaemia is simply self-discipline in the use of words. Ambiguity can often be dispelled by means of distinctions, amplifications and definitions. Lastly, the existence in the legal system of a tradition of using loose concepts—

part of what Max Weber described as "formal rationality"—regulates the exercise of the residual discretion to some extent.

These problems can arise in any use of language. In legislation, the language used must not only communicate the law which is itself an abstraction—a norm contingent on a hypothesis, but it must also delimit the scope of the law. In other words, it must, in its general terms, be capable of embracing a myriad of particular future factual circumstances. The techniques used in the past in this country have been detailed draftsmanship, so that a statute even on a relatively trivial matter has tended to become a labyrinth of distinctions, amplifications and definitions. In some civil law countries, particularly France, however, the tendency has been to legislate at a greater level of generality leaving it to the courts to fill in the details. Thus in French civil law the main principles of the law of torts are contained in five articles whereas in German law there are over twenty articles and the draft code of torts which Sir Frederick Pollock drafted for India ran into some hundreds of sections.[10] The form of drafting is something to which we shall return later in this chapter.

Such defects as we have considered so far are inherent in language or at least in our use of it. The strains and stresses that law-making puts on language can easily become flaws and cracks unless statutes are interpreted with common sense. Again, some philosophers debate not only what common sense is, but even whether it exists at all. Nevertheless, although we may not necessarily be able to define it, like the proverbial elephant, at least we know it when we see it and in the past it has sometimes been missing from judicial interpretation of statutes. We shall now consider how this came about and how the Law Commissions have attempted to tackle the problem.

Interpretation of Statutes

Sir Matthew Hale in his *History of the Common Law* written in the seventeenth century defined legislation in the following terms "... statute laws ... are originally reduced into writing, before they are enacted or receive any binding power: every such law being in the first instance formally drawn up in writing, and made as it were a tripartite indenture, between the King, the Lords and Commons...."[11] It is to be noted that Hale compared a statute with an indenture. He did not say a statute was an indenture. The form of legislation had changed considerably in the period before Hale; originally taking the form of a royal text to which eventually more formalities were attached and to which the acquiescence of the Lords and Commons became essential.[12] The *Prince's Case*[13] in 1605 decided by Coke and his brother judges and reported in Coke's Reports collates much of the ancient learning on the topic. Statutes emerged as documents *sui generis* both in the formalities attendant on their creation and in their effect as the supreme source of law. Once these matters became settled and judges had ceased to be members of the King's Council, there grew up rules of interpretation of statutes in addition to the ordinary common law rules which applied to documents.[14] The Mischief Rule laid down in *Heydon's Case*[15] in 1584 bore considerable affinity to the Equity of Statute idea which prevailed on the Continent[16] and was really pronounced before the supremacy of legislation was finally established. Later, although *Heydon's Case* continued to be cited, the English courts tended to adopt what became known as the Literal Rule relying or at least professing to rely solely on the plain words of the statute.[17] Later still, however, a third rule grew up bearing an ill-defined relationship with the other two. This was the Golden Rule aimed at avoiding inconsistency or great absurdity and inconvenience in legislation.[18] This unholy trinity of vague

and ill-defined rules has received much criticism. Amongst
the judiciary they have appeared at times to be more slogans
than rules, used by the judge dialectically to justify decisions.[19]

One of the most articulate, yet at the same time constructive criticisms of the Rules was made by Professor
Harold Laski in his Note appended as Annex V to the
Report of the Committee on Ministers' Powers in 1932.[20]
The Rules were, he said, defective in a number of particulars;
(1) they exaggerated the degree to which the intention of
Parliament could be discovered from the words of a statute;
(2) they under-estimated the degree to which the "inarticulate
major premiss" of a judge played in determining Parliament's
intention; (3) they exaggerated the certainty and universality
of the common law as a body of principles applicable in the
absence of statute to all possible cases; (4) they cut down
the judge's ability to apply the rules in *Heydon's Case*. Recent
tendencies have been for the judges to attempt to resolve
some of the difficulties arising from the Rules.[21] Progress
has been slow. Academic criticism has increased in the Commonwealth and the United States although comparatively
little has been written by English authors.[22] Nevertheless,
the English Law Commission, realising the necessity of more
sensible and coherent rules,[23] prepared a report on the subject. At the time of writing little has been written on the
report.

The Law Commissions' Report[24]

The Law Commission in Chapter II (on The Scope and
Nature of the Problem) stressed the number of cases before
the courts which involved statutory interpretation.[25] At the
same time they emphasised that a statute is not exclusively
a communication between the legislature and the courts but
also to audiences of varying extent. The intelligibility of

statutes from the point of view of ordinary citizens could not be divorced from the rules of interpretation followed by the courts since the ability to understand a statute depended in the ultimate analysis on intelligent anticipation of the way it would be interpreted by the courts.

It was manifest from the outset that there was no single panacea. There was some justification for the view commonly expressed particularly by judges that statutory interpretation was an art or, as some prefer to put it, a craft. However, the Commission did not share the view sometimes ascribed to the Realists that it was not what the courts said but what they did that mattered. They stressed the effect on the marginal case, the tendency of the present rules to confuse and prolong the trial of the real issues and the general uncertainty pervading the present system.

The problems of interpretation of statutes were common to every advanced community and much could be learned from Commonwealth, American and Continental experience, subject to caveats as to the role of the Constitution in the United States and differing attitudes to codes and the absence of a body of common law in the civil law countries.[26]

The Commission examined the rules and presumptions and found them wanting.[27] The Literal Rule assumed an unattainable perfection in draftsmanship and ignored the limitations of language. It afforded no help where, as was the case, the statute left to the court a limited creative role within the limits set by the general policy of the statute. The Commission felt that an undue emphasis on the literal meaning of words was undesirable and referred to the more liberal approach of the American courts. The Golden Rule set a purely negative standard by reference to absurdity, inconsistency or inconvenience, but provided no clear means to test the existence of these characteristics or measure their quality or extent. On closer examination the Golden Rule turned out to be a less explicit form of the Mischief Rule.

The Commission on the whole thought that the Mischief

Rule was a more satisfactory approach but suffered from certain defects. First, it reflected a very different constitutional balance between the executive, Parliament and the public than would now be acceptable. Secondly, it did not make it clear to what extent the judges should consider the actual language. Thirdly, it assumed that legislation was subsidiary or supplemental to the common law, whereas in modern conditions many statutes represent a fresh departure. Lastly, the rule was laid down before the rules governing the inadmissibility of extrinsic evidence were developed.

With regard to presumptions, the Commission emphasised that a judge was not effectively bound by them since:

- (a) there was no established order of precedence in case of conflict;
- (b) the presumptions were often of doubtful status or imprecise scope;
- (c) the court could decide without reference to the presumptions at all;
- (d) there was no accepted test for resolving a conflict between a presumption and the purpose of an Act.

The Commission thought, however, that a general classification of presumptions would not be practicable. Nevertheless, they favoured action in three areas, mental element in statutory offences (which was being dealt with in a separate report), remedies for breach of statutory duty and in relation to treaties. The latter two will be dealt with below.

The Commission considered the question of the context of a statute.[28] As regards the context provided by the statute the Commission thought that the courts should be able to consider the meaning of the provisions of an Act in the context of short titles, headings and marginal notes but that the weight to be given might often be slight in relation to other more compelling contexts. As regards contexts outside the statute the main factors were relevance, reliability and availability of such materials. On balance, the Commission rejected the admissibility of the parliamentary history of a statute but favoured the use in certain cases of an explanatory memorandum which could be amended with the Bill and submitted to Parliament on the Third Reading of the Bill.[29] The Tudor alternative of a long preamble was considered unsuitable.

To sum up, the Commission drew the following basic conclusions.[30] First, the meaning of a provision in a statute is the meaning which it bears in the light of its intended context. Secondly, in ascertaining the intended context of a provision reference may be made not only to ordinary use of words and grammar, but also to certain other assumptions on the basis of which the legislator may have made the provision. There should not be undue emphasis on the Literal Rule, at the expense of the Mischief Rule or general legislative purpose of an Act or the international obligation which underlay the Act.

The Commission favoured a limited degree of statutory intervention for four purposes. These were:

(a) to clarify and relax in some respects the strict rules as to context;
(b) to emphasise the importance in interpretation of (i) general legislative purpose; and (ii) fulfilment of international obligations;
(c) to indicate whether there is a remedy for breach of statutory obligation; and
(d) to encourage the preparation in selected cases of explanatory material for use by the courts.

Appendix A set out draft clauses to enact their proposals and will be considered in detail below.

This is clearly a matter of crucial importance for any programme of law reform and the Report is a useful survey of many of the problems together with some sensible solutions.

It is a pity, however, that more general attention was not

given to the role of language in law making.[31] As a matter of theory it seems that the legal profession continues to reject current philosophical approaches to the meaning of words in favour of various forms of essentialism. Statutes often set out the "essence" for the purpose of that piece of legislation. Where this is not the case lawyers and the courts tend to resort to a *genus et differentia* approach to the elucidation of meaning and to limit the context of a word to be examined. Can it be that current philosophical methods are only really useful with the vaguer concepts in jurisprudence and too impracticable for the legal profession in its daily wrestling with the meaning of words?[32] The Report does not consider the matter from this angle at all nor the attendant problems of ambiguity and change of meaning in any detail.[33] In view of the recent work in linguistic philosophy and semantics and the attempts by people like Naom Chomsky to reduce language to an empirical study this would seem an eminently suitable topic for research by the new Institute of Socio-legal Studies in Oxford, where social scientists might add a little empiricism to the speculations of linguistically minded jurisprudes and perhaps carry Wittgenstein to his logical conclusion[34]—a sociology of language.

The Report does not properly analyse the respective roles of Parliament and the courts in legislation in any depth. The late Professor Hart and Dean Sacks made some useful comments on the futility of a search for the purpose of a statute and the need for "attribution of purpose."[35] This is particularly important where by the use of "open textured" words Parliament has deliberately left the courts a creative role. It is also important as a general approach where the judicial role is not so obvious. Seeds of this can be seen in the Equity of a Statute approach of the Tudor judges.[36] It is a pity that this doctrine was not further developed in English law.[37] The recent case of *Jones* v. *Secretary of State for Social Services*[38] in 1972 does, however, show that the judges are prepared to adopt a more purposive approach to the in-

terpretation of statutes and in that respect at least the Report
can be said to have been implemented by judicial legislation.

Although the explanatory memorandum appears somewhat as an innovation, it was in fact suggested as a possibility
by Professor Laski in 1932.[39] On the basis of the present
Report, it is easy to see difficulties arising where there is a
conflict between an Act and such a memorandum. The
Report gives little guidance on resolving such a conflict.[40]
It would seem that the wording of the statute should prevail
and this is in fact all that Professor Laski suggested in 1932.
As regards the other documents draft clauses 1(b) (d) and (e)
are expressed in wide terms and would be wide enough to
include ministerial white papers. It would seem wrong that
a white paper setting out in political terms the broad aims
of a government policy, often in vague language, should be
allowed to determine the precise legal effect of the legislation.
At the same time it also seems paradoxical that such documents should be allowed when reports of parliamentary
proceedings are not to be allowed since the latter provides
a necessary connecting link. It is submitted that a specially
prepared explanatory memorandum revised during the
parliamentary passage of a statute is preferable to such
documents.

The admissibility of such a document was, however, rig-
orously attacked by the General Council of the Bar in a
memorandum to the Lord Chancellor.[41] The memorandum
opened with a reference to Lord Halsbury's Introduction to
the first edition of Halsbury's *Laws of England* where he
said "A passage appears to be obscure: let it be cleared up
rather by alteration than by comment: retrench, add, sub-
tract as much as you will, but never explain. By the latter
certainty will generally, perspicuity and brevity will always
suffer. The more words there are, the more words are there
about which doubts may be entertained." At first sight this
sounds very convincing but when considered would seem to

render the use of definitions otiose. Also the luxury of alteration of statutes is not too easily afforded.

As for the detailed objections of the Bar Council most of them are of a high level of generality bordering on the *a priori*, fobbed off as statements of future fact which it is impossible to confirm or refute. First it is said that the ordinary citizen to whom a statute is directed will be able to place less reliance on the wording of the statute. But does "the ordinary citizen" read statutes? It is submitted that it is the extraordinary citizen who reads them—the professional in the course of his professional role. Ordinary citizens tend to rely at present on government literature explaining the legislation. Secondly it is said that recourse to lawyers will have to be more frequent. Surely this is on the face of it a paradoxical point for a body of lawyers to take. The paradox is, however, resolved by the third point. Recourse to lawyers will be more expensive because they will have to consider more material. This appears to be the real bone of contention. Then it is said that draftsmen are likely to increase the degree of uncertainty for they will no longer be faced with a situation where the language used is paramount. In other words the standards of draftsmanship will decline. Surely this is a libel on members of their own profession, wholly untrue and unjustified. There was, in the Bar Council's view, no evidence that a significant number of wrong decisions had resulted from the present state of the law or that the proposals would reduce whatever number of wrong decisions there may be. Nor was there any evidence that the proposals would render the solution of problems less costly. On the contrary not only would the solution of problems be more costly but because there are more words about which doubts might be ascertained there would be more problems. It would seem implicit in the reasoning of the Bar Council that they recognise that there are some wrong decisions but that these are not significant. What significance means in this context we do not know. Again we are met with vague and sweeping generalisations about the future which one can neither confirm nor refute.

On the other hand the Bar Council supported the recommendations on punctuations, sidenotes and headings. The Bar Council's basic hostility to the Report manifested itself again in connexion with the Matrimonial Proceedings and Property Bill and the Animals Bill where they attacked proposed relaxation of the extrinsic evidence rule.

However, notwithstanding the Bar Council's objections it would seem that with the United Kingdom's entry into the Common Market the Law Commissions' recommendations probably do not go far enough and this is probably the principal reason why they have not been implemented. Also section 3 of the European Communities Act 1972 would appear to allow any document published in the Official Journal to be admissible. Indeed the section puts judges on judicial notice of them. It is suggested that the Law Commission need to publish a revised report in the light of these changes. As it is, section 3 has just added to the growing chaos of the existing rules and created an unfortunate distinction between Common Market and non-Common Market law. Also the Vienna Convention on the Law of Treaties which has been ratified by the United Kingdom goes further in the admission of extrinsic evidence.

Some of the draft clauses set out in Appendix A of the Law Commissions' Report are badly worded. Thus in clause 1(2) the weight to be given to intrinsic and extrinsic materials listed in 1(1) "shall be no more than is appropriate in the circumstances." This negative test confers a positive discretion on the courts. Should not the Commission have cut this down in some way to ensure that the courts followed its recommendations? It is suggested that a statute enacting the draft clauses should incorporate the Report. Clause 2 states that construction to promote the general legislative purpose and fulfil international obligations "shall be included among the principles to be applied in the interpretation of

Acts." What does "included" mean here? What has happened to the unholy trinity, the Mischief, Literal and Golden Rules? Are they abolished? If so, why not do so expressly? Also, what happens where statutes conflict or where there are competing international obligations? Again, the Report is silent.

Overall, it does seem a little ironic that in its Report on Interpretation of Statutes the Commission has left the wording of its draft clauses so vague and incomplete. After all in relation to words "The question is," said Humpty Dumpty, "which is to be master—that's all."[42]

The Form of Legislation

Closely related to the question of interpretation is the question of the form of statutes which the Law Commissions are apparently considering but did not discuss in the Report.

Why, for instance, should parliamentary draftsmen almost always try to reduce everything to words? Some matters could be better represented in mathematical formulae which would be more intelligible in the context of tax legislation than a morass of complicated language. Their use in the capital gains provisions of the Finance Acts seems to have been successful. This would be better still if an example was given to be worked out in figures. As we shall see, examples (albeit verbal ones) were used in some of the Indian codes and there was distinguished support for their widespread use in legislation. In some cases diagrams would be useful—for example, in Factory Acts legislation. The recent report of the Robens Committee[43] highlights the unsatisfactory nature of the present safety legislation, although their solution is fairly moderate—a general enabling Act setting out the main duties supplemented by Statutory Instruments drafted in more intelligible language.

Another recent suggestion has been the use of flow charts

or algorithms which enable an individual applying the rules to trace the circumstances of his particular case through to a conclusion by adopting the appropriate alternative in each case.[44]

As Sir Leslie Scarman's public utterances have shown, the Law Commissions have all this in mind. So far we merely have a loose-leaf statute book appearing, mitigating the deplorable tendency of legislation by reference but Sir Leslie has suggested at times that we ought as a matter of general administrative machinery to have a Ministry of Justice charged with the task of supervising the form and quality of legislation.[45]

In the meantime, however, parliamentary committees have been considering the Process of Legislation[46] and Delegated Legislation in the period 1970 to 1972.[47] The recent outcome of the former has been (ironically but perhaps inevitably) the proliferation of a further committee on the Preparation of Legislation. Its terms of reference are: "With a view to achieving greater simplicity and clarity in statute law, to review the form in which public Bills are drafted, excluding consideration of matters relating to policy formulation and the legislative programme; to consider any consequential implications for Parliamentary procedure; and to make recommendations." The Chairman is the Rt. Hon. Sir David Renton Q.C., M.P., a former Minister of State at the Home Office with more than twenty-seven years experience of Parliament, who had submitted a memorandum to the Select Committee on Procedure and given evidence before it. The composition of his committee is interesting. The English and Scottish Law Commissions are represented in the form of Sir Samuel Cooke, Sir Noel Hutton Q.C. who was First Parliamentary Counsel from 1956-1968 and is working at the Law Commission on the Landlord and Tenant Code, Mr. Ewan Stewart Q.C., a member of the Scottish Law Commission and former Solicitor-General of Scotland and Sir John Gibson Q.C., Counsel to the Scottish Law Commission and Scottish parliamentary draftsman from 1961-71. The remainder of the committee consists of the Rt. Hon. Baroness Bacon, former Labour M.P. and Minister of State at the Home Office, Clerks of Bills from both Houses of Parliament, practitioners in the form of Mr. J. A. R. Finlay Q.C. and Mr. S. J. Mosley, a solicitor; a senior civil servant, Sir Basil Engholm; Mr. Ivor Richard Q.C., Labour M.P.; Sir Patrick Macrory, a Northern Ireland industrialist who has served on recent government committees in Northen Ireland and lastly the Duke of Atholl, printer, newspaper publisher and member of the Red Deer Commission. The secretary is a member of the Cabinet Office which suggests perhaps a subtle way in which the Prime Minister intends to keep an eye on the activities of the committee.

Experience tends to inhibit enthusiasm at the creation of a committee and overall the membership of this particular one is weighted towards people who are likely to have a conservative and "establishment" approach. Nevertheless at the very least it is a cautious step in the right direction and is a welcome break in that it allows outsiders to examine critically the holiest of parliamentary holies. Whether this will result in iconoclasm remains to be seen.

Consolidation and Codification

These are, of course, major items on the Commissions' agenda. In the United Kingdom consolidation means the process whereby a new statute re-enacts the contents of many earlier statutes with only such alterations as are necessary to produce a coherent whole. It is a fallacy to assume that the task is merely mechanical. In the words of Sir Courtenay Ilbert[48] "The work of consolidation involves re-writing, not merely planning together, of laws, the substitution of modern for antiquated language and machinery, the harmonising of inconsistent enactments and yet the per-

formance of this work in such a way as to effect the minimum
of change in expressions which have been made the subject
of judicial decisions and on which a long course of practice
has been based." The aim is not only to reduce the confusion
on the Statute Book but also to mitigate the disadvantages
inherent in legislation by reference.[49]

The cause of consolidation attracts widespread sympathy.[50]
We have seen how, as long ago as Bacon, there had been a
call for consolidation. Bentham had repeated the call in the
nineteenth century. It received some support in the Report
of the Select Committee of the House of Commons set up
in 1875 to consider "whether and what means can be adopted
to improve the manner and language of current legislation."
In this century, Viscount Jowitt was a particularly strong
supporter and so far the Law Commissions have achieved
considerable success.

Codification on the other hand is a rather more polemical
topic.[51] To an English lawyer a code can be basically defined
as "enactment which sums up in theory not only any prev-
iously existing legislation, but also the common law and
equity governing the topic."[52]

Opinions have, however, differed in the past on the precise
form this should take. The two basic patterns are the French
Code Civil which avoids definitions and favours broad principles leaving it to the courts to fill in the gaps in fact if
not in theory and the German civil code which is more
detailed and attempts to be more definitive. Bentham's conception appears to have been of a code based on an elaborate
digest of existing law subdivided into particular subjects
with the deadwood removed.[53] This was the conception of
a code adopted by Stephen, Chalmers and Pollock for English
law in the nineteenth century. The codes drafted for India
also incorporated factual examples and the use of such examples was favoured by Bentham, Austin, Macaulay[54] and
Pollock.[55] The use of illustrations was explained by Macaulay
in a letter to Lord Auckland prefixed to the draft Indian

Penal Code.[56] They would, he thought, greatly facilitate the understanding of the law and often serve as a defence of the law. There were two things which a legislature should always have in view when framing laws—first that they should as far as possible be precise, secondly that they should be easily understood. To combine the two was often impossible. Macaulay thought the method they adopted was the best—"We have, in framing our definitions, thought principally of making them precise, and have not shrunk from rugged or intricate phraseology when such phraseology appeared to us to be necessary to precision. If it appeared to us that our language was likely to perplex an ordinary reader, we added as many illustrations as we thought necessary for the purpose of explaining it. The definitions and enacting clauses contain the whole law. The illustrations make nothing law which would not be law without them. They only exhibit the law in full action and show what its effects will be on the events of common life."

Thus the code is a Statute Book and a collection of decided cases but with the advantage over ordinary case law that they are decided by the legislation.

A more elaborate form of code was suggested by Mr. F. Vaughan Hawkins in a paper on Codification delivered to the Juridical Society in 1865.[57] In his view, a perfect code should contain first, the rules of law, with explanations, definitions, exceptions and qualifications; secondly, examples of the application of the rules and thirdly reasons for the rules, i.e. the *rationes legis* as opposed to the *rationes decidendi*. Hawkins seems to have been alone in his third requirement although Bentham was in favour of the occasional sprinkling of moral exhortations to leaven the provisions of a code.

The Law Commissions, while not tying themselves to a particular form of code, are committed at least to considering codifying substantial areas of English and Scots law.[58] It will be useful, therefore, to consider briefly some of the arguments for and against codification.

The main argument traditionally used, and frequently used by the Law Commissions, is the great bulk and unwieldiness of the present law.[59] It is argued that a code would produce in its place systematic, compact and accessible law. The law would then be more accessible to the public, even if not necessarily completely intelligible to them.[60] Case law produces gaps, uncertainties and irrational distinctions which a code would remove. Also it has been argued that the common law has not in recent times been able to adapt itself quickly enough to changing conditions.[61] This has been particularly true in the field of contract.

Against these are a number of arguments which were put forward in the nineteenth century and have been re-iterated recently. First it is said that a code is necessarily incomplete and cannot provide for all future cases.[62] The easiest way of meeting this criticism is to recognise its partial truth and compare this with the existing law. Then it is argued that a code is difficult to alter.[63] In this country there is no reason why this should be so. Parliament will not abdicate its legislative functions once a code has been enacted, the judges will continue to interpret and create law by analogy and the Law Commissions will presumably continue in business.

Next, it is said that the common law is more malleable. Although there is some force in this criticism it is tempered to a certain extent by the doctrine of precedent. Again, it is said that a code is more likely to engender competitions of competing analogies than the common law. This obviously depends on the quality of draftsmanship and might arise if the drafting of codes for different areas of law was in different hands and was not adequately supervised.

Another argument is that the legal textbooks perform the function of a code but these are clearly not authoritative unless and until they are archaic.

It is also argued that a code in order to approach completeness must consist of rules so minute and numerous that no man can learn or retain them, and that in any event, it is impossible to provide completely for future particular cases. The answer to this is that one has a choice as regards the subject matter of a code and as regards its form, it should not aim at a specification of cases but providing a series of rules applicable to cases.

More major criticisms are those of Savigny[64] who attacked the codification movement in Germany in the nineteenth century and argued that a code will not be fitted to the customs and experience of the community, the *Volksgeist*, and will destroy continuity in legal development. Apart from the inherent vagueness of the concept of the *Volksgeist*, there is no reason why a code which restates English law which has developed over centuries and which is kept up-to-date by a body such as the Law Commission should not fit the changing needs of society.

Lastly, we have the brunt of Professor Hahlo's powerful criticism in an article in the *Modern Law Review* in 1967, dramatically entitled, "Here lies the Common Law: Rest in Peace."[65] It did not seem unlikely to him (to employ his double negative) that as a result of codification the influence of English law outside the United Kingdom would decrease. It will suffer a *capitus deminutio* being reduced in status from the senior member of the Anglo-American common law family to that of a purely national system governed by just one code among many. He asked rhetorically "will America succeed England as the chief custodian of the Common Law?" Professor Gower, by way of rejoinder,[66] argued that America had nearly done so already because of its use of the Restatements and the Model and Uniform codes which rendered its unwieldy mass of case law more easily ascertainable. We could be more helpful to other members of the Anglo-American family by our work in law reform and codification.

To sum up, the Law Commission has shown an awareness that all is not well in the present form of legislation but so far it has failed to provide much in the way of concrete proposals.[67] Its Joint Report on Interpretation of Statutes has not been implemented save in a limited way by the suggestion of a different approach on the part of some of the judiciary. The new Committee on the Preparation of Legislation may have some influence on the creation of more rational parliamentary procedures and in the style of legislative drafting but on the face of it it looks rather a conservative body. The presence of outsiders particularly representatives of the two Law Commissions, however, is to be welcomed. The quiet, undramatic but nevertheless valuable work of consolidation and statute law revision has continued under the Law Commission. As to the wisdom of codification opinions clearly differ and the arguments for and against are generally of a high level of generality which are difficult to prove or refute scientifically. Also the debate is necessarily inconclusive because of the apparent lack of decision by the Law Commission as to the form the codes should take. The choice of the law of contract as a suitable case for treatment is the most controversial of the areas chosen and there are hints of second thoughts by at least some of the new commissioners. Whether it will be abandoned remains to be seen.[68]

Notes

[1] Scarman, *Law Reform—The New Pattern*, p. 17. Lord Devlin, however, considered that the Law Commission should have a sort of delegated legislative power to make law so as to carry out forthwith at least its more detailed suggestions for the removal of anomalies in the field of lawyer's law. See the "Process of Law Reform" in (1966) 63 L.S.Gaz. 333. Contrast the idea canvassed by R. J. Sutton in "The English Law Commission: a new philosophy of Law Reform" (1967) 20 Vanderbilt L.R. 1009, 1019 that the law Commission should address its reports to the judiciary to enable some reforms to be promoted by judicial legislation.

[2] See W. H. Loyd "The Equity of a Statute" in 58 Univ. of Penn. L.R. 76 and Professor S. E. Thorne's introduction to *A Discourse upon the Exposicion and Understandinge of Statutes.*

[3] *Principles of Human Knowledge*, 1st ed., Introduction, sec. 21. *Cf.* Locke, *Essay Concerning Human Understanding*, Bk. 3, Chap. XI, sec. 4.

[4] *Ethics*, Bk. Five, Chap. 10.

[5] *The Labyrinth of Language*, pp. 162-3.

[6] This is Roquentin's fate in Sartre's *La Nausée*.

[7] See generally Black, *op. cit.*, p. 170 *et seq.*

[8] See Black's Chapter II "Vagueness: an exercise in logical analysis" in *Language and Philosophy*; H. L. A. Hart, *The Concept of Law*, Chap. VII and the other works listed by Hart on p. 249.

[9] See Charles P. Curtis, *It's Your Law*, p. 76.

[10] See Generally F. H. Lawson, *A Common Lawyer looks at the Civil Law*, Chap. II.

[11] *History of the Common Law*, p. 82.

[12] See T. F. T. Plucknett, *Legislation of Edward I*, pp. 11 *et seq.*

[13] (1605) 8 Rep. 1—see especially 20.

[14] See 2 Coke's Inst., Proeme and 1 Bl. Comm. 85 (10th edition).

[15] (1584) 3 Co. Rep. 7a.

[16] See generally the learned introduction by Professor Samuel E. Thorne to *A Discourse upon the Exposicion and Understandinge of Statutes* taken from Lord Ellesmere's *Commonplace book.*

[17] See the Law Commission's Report on Interpretation of Statutes (hereinafter called "the Report") Law Com. No. 21, p. 20.

[18] See the Report, Chap. IV and the authorities there cited.

[19] See *e.g.* Odger's *Construction of Deeds and Statutes* (5th ed. by Prof. G. Dworkin), p. 451.

[20] Cmd. 4060 (1932), pp. 135 *et seq.*

[21] The Report, p. 7.

[22] See the literature listed in Appendix C to the Report, esp. D. J. Ll. Davies, "The Interpretation of Statutes in the Light of their Policy by the English Courts" (1935) 35 Col. L.R. 519; J. Willis "Statute Interpretation in a Nutshell" (1938) 16 C.B.R. 1; F. Frankfurter, "Some Reflections on the Reading of Statutes" (1947) 47 Col. L.R. 527 and D. Payne, "The Intention of the Legislature in the Interpretation of Statutes" [1956] C.L.P. 96.

[23] Item XVII of the Law Commission's first programme. See also Sir Leslie Scarman, in *Law Reform—the New Pattern*, the Lindsay Memorial Lectures delivered at the University of Keele in 1967, at p. 17, where he said "In a sense, the Commission has a vested interest in enacted law; it cannot as judges do, mould and develop the law by day to day decision. Its reputation will stand or fall by the contributions it makes to enacted law." See also p. 49: "The reality is that we are already governed by statute supplemented by the Common Law." See also (and this is not wholly a facetious reference), St. Thomas More's *Utopia*, translated by Paul Turner, p. 106.

[24] See H. Bloom's note in (1970) 33 M.L.R. 197; see also 119 New L.J. 565 and 587 and "The Interpretation of Statutes" an article

in 54 *Law Guardian* 11, following the Bar Council's memorandum which is discussed later.

[25] See the analysis of reported cases in n. 2 on p. 3 of the Report.

[26] See generally Chapter III.

[27] See Chapter IV.

[28] See Chapter V.

[29] See Chapter VI.

[30] See Chapter IV.

[31] But see Sir Leslie Scarman's *Law Reform—the New Pattern*, pp. 56-57 for his useful remarks.

[32] Clearly the practitioner and the jurisprude are engaged in different functions with words. It is arguable that these different functions require different methods of approach. *Cf.* H. L. A. Hart, "Definition and Theory of Jurisprudence" (1954) 70 L.Q.R. 37 but see also R. Summers' introduction to *Essays in Legal Philosophy*, pp. 2 *et seq.*

[33] See G. C. Thornton, *Legislative Drafting*, pp. 9-17 and Julius Stone, *Legal Systems and Lawyers' Reasonings*, pp. 29 *et seq.*

[34] See generally Ernest Gellner, *Words and Things*.

[35] See the tentative edition of their work *The Legal Process* and Bloom's note in (1970) 33 M.L.R. 197, 200-01. See also "Codification and Judge-made Law—A problem of co-existence"—a lecture given by Sir Leslie Scarman to the Faculty of Law of the University of Birmingham.

[36] See Coke, 1 Inst. 24 and Plowden's note to *Eyston* v. *Studd* (1574) Plow. 459, 465. See also W. H. Loyd, "The Equity of the Statute" in 58 Univ. of Penn. L.R. 76 and S. E. Thorne's introduction to *A Discourse upon the Exposicion and Understandinge of Statutes* and "The Equity of a Statute and Heydon's Case" in 31 Illinois L.R. 202.

[37] See Sir Fortunatus Dwarris's *A General Treatise on Statutes*, Vol. II, p. 721, for a contrary view and *Craies on Statute Law* (7th ed.), p. 102 for authorities hostile to the idea. Lord Denning (ever resourceful) attempted resuscitation of the idea in *Magor & St Mellons R.D.C.* v. *Newport Corp.* [1950] 2 All E.R. 1226, 1236 only to be accused by Lord Simonds in the House of Lords of "a naked usurpation of the legislative function under the thin disguise of interpretation" [1952] A.C. at pp. 190-91. Lord Denning recanted in *London Transport Executive* v. *Betts* [1959] A.C. 213, 247. The idea, however, received some measured support from Lord Evershed in his Maccabaean Lecture in Jurisprudence, "The Impact of Statute on the Law of England," in *Proceedings of the British Academy* (1956) at pp. 258, 260, 262.

[38] [1972] 1 All E.R. 145. See also *Kammins Ballrooms Co. Ltd.* v. *Zenith Investments Ltd.* [1970] 2 All E.R. 871 especially per Lord Diplock at pp. 891 *et seq.* In *Wachtel* v. *Wachtel* [1973] Fam 72, Lord Denning M.R., delivering the judgment of the court after referring to the Law Commission's Report on Financial Provision in Matrimonial Proceedings said, "It has sometimes been suggested

that we should not have regard to the reports of the Law Commission which lead to legislation: but we think we should. They are most helpful in showing the mischief which Parliament intended to remedy."

[39] Cmd. 4060 (1932), p. 136.

[40] ". . . it would be no more binding on the courts than other contextual material"—see the Report, pp. 41-42.

[41] See the outline in 54 *Law Guardian* 11.

[42] Lewis Carrol, *Through the Looking-Glass*, Chap. VI.

[43] *Safety and Health at Work* Cmnd. 5034, (1972), pp. 7 *et seq.*

[44] See F. A. R. Bennion, *Tangling with the Law,* pp. 14 *et seq.* These are used already in the Civil Service.

[45] See Scarman, *Law Reform—the New Pattern,* p. 41. See further the two reports of the Statute Law Society, *Statute Law Deficiencies* and *Statute Law—the Key to Clarity,* in particular the exchange of correspondence between the Society and Sir Leslie Scarman which appears in the appendices.

[46] Second Report from the Select Committee on Procedure 1970-71. This Committee also recommended (*inter alia*) the regular use of pre- and post-legislation committees.

[47] Report from the Joint Committee on Delegated Legislation 1971-72. H.C. 475/43d. See (1973) 70 L.S.Gaz. 1879.

[48] *Legislative Methods and Forms,* pp. 112-13.

[49] See *Statute Law: the Key to Clarity,* for the arguments in favour of textual amendments.

[50] See generally "Statute Law Revision and Consolidation"—the address of Viscount Jowitt L.C. to the Holdsworth Club in 1951.

[51] See R. Pound, *Jurisprudence,* Vol. 3, pt. 5, pp. 675-738 and the references cited there. For recent contributions to the debate see Sir Leslie Scarman's "A Code of English Law?"—a lecture given to the University of Hull in 1966; H. R. Hahlo's "Here lies the Common Law: Rest in Peace" in (1967) 30 M.L.R. 241; L. C. B. Gower's Comment, *ibid.,* at p. 259 and Aubrey L. Diamond's "Codification of the Law of Contract" in (1968) 31 M.L.R. 361.

[52] F. H. Lawson in (1960) 2 *Inter-American Law Review,* 1-3. See also R. Floyd Clarke, *The Science of Law and Law Making,* p. 10.

[53] See Clarke, *op. cit.,* p. 281.

[54] See the Anglo Indian Codes (ed. Whitley Stokes), Vol. 1, pp. xxiii-xxvii.

[55] See introduction to *A Digest of the Law of Partnership* (1877), pp. viii *et seq.*

[56] See Whitley Stokes, *op. cit.*

[57] See 3 *Juridical Society Papers* 110, 112 and Clarke, *op. cit.,* pp. 282 *et seq.*

[58] First programme (Law Com. No. 1)—codification of the law of contract, landlord and tenant and family law. Second programme (Law Com. No. 14)—criminal law.

[59] See generally J. Austin's *Jurisprudence*, Vol. II, Notes on Codification, pp. 1056 *et seq.* and Diamond, *op. cit.*, pp. 263 *et seq.* for a valuable summary of the arguments together with useful data of authorities cited in recent cases and knowledge of the law by the public.

[60] See D. Lloyd in (1949) 2 C.L.P. at p. 165. *Cf.* Hahlo, *op. cit.*, p. 245 and D. M. Walker "Reform, Restatement and the Law Commissions" (1965) *Juridical Review* 245, 247-248

[61] See Sutton, *op. cit.*, p. 1014; Gower, *op. cit.*, p. 259.

[62] See Savigny, *Vom Beruf unserer Zeit für Gesetzgebung und Rechtswissenschaft*, p. 24; Clarke, *op. cit.*, pp. 39-40.

[63] Hahlo, *op. cit.*, pp. 250-51.

[64] *Op. cit.*

[65] *Op cit.*, pp. 258-59.

[66] *Ibid.*, p. 262.

[67] This has been conceded by Sir Leslie Scarman in an interview in (1973) 70 L.S.Gaz. 1345.

[68] On July 9, 1973 Lord Gardiner asked the Lord Chancellor for a statement of the progress of the Law Commission's examination of the law of contract with a view to codification. Lord Hailsham replied "The examination is proceeding but the Law Commission have decided with my approval that a change is required in their method of work. They propose to publish a series of Working Papers on particular parts of the law of contract. This will simplify consultation and help their consideration of proposed reforms. Work on a draft code will be suspended in the meantime, but the Commission will again consider codification when they have completed the work which they are now putting in hand." *Hansard*, House of Lords, Monday July 9, 1973, cols. 624-25.

CHAPTER 6

LAW REFORM, PUBLIC OPINION AND THE UNDERLYING PROBLEM OF VALUES

IN a modern democratic society it is almost axiomatic that there is a close but complex relationship between law, public opinion and morality and that there is a constant dynamic tension between them.[1]

Thus although law tends as a whole to reflect many aspects of so-called public opinion and to change with it, there are other times when law itself changes public opinion or at least is used to attempt to change public opinion, as for instance with race relations. There are times when law defies a substantial volume of public opinion—possible examples might be the abolition of the death penalty, the Industrial Relations Act 1971 and the European Communities Act 1972. There are also, of course, many situations where the law must postulate rules where there is no clear guide from public opinion, as for instance many rules in real property.

In this chapter we shall attempt an analysis of only a small part of the overall relationship—the role of public opinion and public and private value judgments in law reform.

First, however, let us analyse the nature of public opinion in a little more detail. Opinion is distinguished by some political and social scientists[2] from personality attributes and attitudes. Personality refers to those aspects of an individual's orientation to life which are acquired early and are deeply ingrained, a relatively stable compound of genetic endowment and early learning and socialisation. Attitudes are less part of the basic psychological structure of the individual and more reactions to external stimuli as for instance communists, students and the Tory Party. Examples of measures on attitude scales devised by the American sociologist McClosky to test conservative and liberal attitudes include pro-business attitudes and left-wing sympathies. Opinions on the other hand are articulated responses and judgments reacting to particular stimuli which are specific and timebound, *e.g.* a decision, a proposal or a policy.

Public opinion appears to have been first defined by Sir Robert Peel in 1820 as "that great compound of folly, weakness, prejudice, wrong feeling, right feeling, obstinacy, and newspaper paragraphs,"[3] a rather patronising definition which appears to confuse opinion with at least some personality attributes and attitudes and to ignore the question of who constitutes the public. Dicey appeared to adopt this definition with some modifications when he talked about "a body of beliefs, convictions, sentiments, accepted principles or firmly rooted prejudices." He later qualified this to refer to the "wishes and ideas as to legislation held by the majority of those citizens who have at a given moment taken an effective part in public life," *i.e.* what he defined in a word as "legislative" public opinion. Modern social scientists have attacked Dicey for showing no interest in the opinions of the general populace and reflecting "little more than the views of the sharply limited class of intellectuals whose writings directly influence the minds of the nation's legislation."[4]

Yet even in modern sociology there is no hard and fast definition of "public opinion." Some writers attempt to limit this to opinion which in contrast to mass opinion is comparatively stable.[5] This is even more limited a concept than Dicey's and not altogether satisfactory

A working definition might be a judgment held by a sizeable proportion of society resting on grounds insufficient for complete demonstration.[6] This of course begs many questions such as how large a proportion is concerned, how the opinion came to be held, how it is assessable and so on, but it does make one thing clear and that is that it is concerned with something which is a matter of controversy on which knowledge is (at least for the moment) impossible.

Dicey wrote, as we have seen, of public opinion as a body of convictions and beliefs and prejudices as well as what he called crosscurrents due to controversy. Nevertheless one may perhaps logically distinguish between consensus and opinion.[7] Plato confined opinion to that which is subject to change. Opinions are developed about controversial topics whereas in belief or consensus an idea fills the mind to the exclusion of possible alternatives.

Over the last hundred years dogmatic consensus has broken down and made way for relativism. The increasing role of the mass media has popularised the knowledge of the existence of variant beliefs, codes and standards. The areas of certainty have narrowed. "In order to show the variety of all efforts to found rationally an absolute and universal morality, the varieties and contradictions of moral rules recognised at various times and in various societies had to be systematically described."[8] Thus the field of opinion has widened and that of consensus diminished.

One important factor in a causal sense in the formation of public opinion and opinion change is the work of organised groups.[9] Such groups which may broadly be classified into "interest" groups and "cause" groups[10] perform a complex but increasingly influential role in law reform. Indeed some political commentators argue that their existence is a necessary condition for the maintenance of political liberty.[11] Whether this is meant in a logical or an empirical sense is not always made clear.

On many matters they are the only significant public and their work is useful, even essential, to government. Another important feature is that they supply a supplement to the formal constitutional system of territorial representation in national and local government. In these and in other ways pressure groups contribute to the formation of public opinion and to the "search for rationality"[12] in policy-making and law reform. There is not scope in this book to examine the heterogeneity of pressure groups and their effectiveness in the promotion of law reform but simply to note that here lies a valuable field for empirical work in the sociology of law.

Returning to a more analytical plane let us consider another important question, namely what is the nature of the relationship of public opinion to value judgments? The answer at first sight would seem to be that public opinion includes but does not necessarily consist exclusively of commonly held value judgments. However, it must be conceded that the term "value" itself is a loose one. In a broad sense it includes any measure of worth including economic value in capital or labour terms; in a narrower sense it connotes some ethical standard. Like Bentham's conception of a principle it is "something that points out some external consideration, as a means of warranting and guiding the internal sentiments of approbation and disapprobation."[13] Again the term "value judgment," although a very common term, is loosely used. It can connote the act of adopting a particular value or the value itself but is often used to mean something which is simply not an empirical statement of fact. If it is used in the latter broad sense then public opinion consists exclusively of publicly held value judgments.

Probably the best working definition in this context is that adopted by Jacob and Flink in *Values and their Function in Decision-making*, *viz.* "normative standards" (other than law) "by which human beings are influenced in their choice among the alternative courses of action which they perceive."[14] This avoids identifying the concept of values with the moral imperatives operating in a given society or period but limits the concept to the normative.

This question of values raises a fundamental question as

to the role of the Law Commissioners. Can they operate on the basis of their own value judgments or must they only have regard to those expressed in public opinion?

In considering this question with regard to the Law Commissioners one must first look to the Law Commission Act and see the extent of their statutory obligations. In fact the Act is silent on the matter. In section 3, as we have seen, it talks of keeping the law under review with a view to its systematic development and reform and modernisation. It provides for submission of programmes to the Minister and consequently to Parliament. What then is their responsibility? The answer would seem to be that the Commissioners, by analogy with Burke's[15] conception of the role of a Member of Parliament, should give great weight to public opinion but ultimately should not sacrifice their "unbiased opinion,... mature judgement ... and enlightened conscience" to it. Burke said of a Member of Parliament that he owed his constituents "not his industry only, but his judgement; and he betrays, instead of serving you, if he sacrifices it to your opinion." Obviously there are great differences between Law Commissioners and Members of Parliament but it is submitted that ultimately on this particular matter Burke's principle holds true. The Law Commission should and does consult public opinion. In the past it has largely done this by circulating the appropriate pressure groups. The family property survey shows perhaps the beginning of a wider consultation. But ultimately they owe us their judgment. One might of course add that in their case there is the extra safeguard of Parliament in case of possible errors of judgment. Unlike the judiciary their value judgments need to pass the test of Parliament before implementation.

In the remainder of this chapter we will attempt an analysis of some of the social value judgments which they have adopted and the extent to which public opinion was tested and lastly the question of the extent to which the existence of public opinion can be tested and conflicts of values can be resolved.

A statement of the basic general values of the English Law Commission is contained in the First Programme.[16]

They felt that the law should be simpler, more readily accessible, more easily understandable and more certain than it was. Statistics should be interpreted with common sense. A proper balance should be struck between the rule of law and the administrative techniques of a highly developed industrial society. The legal system should be brought into harmony with the social and economic requirements of a modern state. In particular the operation of the legal system should be adjusted to changes in prices, wages and relevant factors affecting the cost of living. Lastly, the legal system should be capable of making a rapid remedial response to defects exposed by judicial comment and other informed criticism.

It can be seen that these show a strong Benthamite influence and represent a twentieth century restatement of utilitarian views. To translate this into modern idiom much of the work of the Law Commissions can be described as "consumer orientated." Throughout its activities, particularly in codification, there is concern for what Edmond Cahn following Llewellyn described as the "law consumer."[17]

Concern for the consumer as product consumer can be seen clearly in the Report on Exemption Clauses in Contracts of Sale of Goods[18] where there are recommendations to limit contracting out of basic obligations. An attempt to define "consumer sales" is made in the draft clauses[19] which have now been implemented in the Supply of Goods (Implied Terms) Act 1973. Further work continues on exclusion clauses generally.

In the field of property law evidence of this acceptance of the value of consumer protection is the report on civil liability of vendors and lessors for defective premises[20] and the support the Law Commission has given to registration of title to land.[21] On other items of property law reform, however, such as the basic question of title,[22] easements[23] and restrictive covenants[24] the position is less clear cut. The Law Commission's role there is to balance conflicting interests of persons at arms length. In any event the major debates in the property field are now in the field of social policy.

In the area of tort there seems to be some movement towards acceptance of the value of strict liability covered by compulsory insurance and a movement away from liability based on fault. In this respect, however, the work of the Law Commissions was frustrated by the refusal of Lord Chancellors Gardiner and Hailsham to give approval under section 3(1)(c) of the Law Commissions Act to an investigation into the principles governing accidents involving personal injury because of the policy issues involved. The effect of this can be clearly seen in the Report on Civil Liability for Dangerous Things and Activities.[25]

However, on December 19, 1972 the Prime Minister announced in the House of Commons that a royal commission was to be set up under Lord Pearson to consider the basis of civil liability for causing death or personal injury. The impetus had been the Report of the Robens Committee on Safety and Health at Work and the concern over the fate of the victims of thalidomide. The matter was obviously considered to raise such fundamental social issues and to be so politically controversial that it was better to refer it to a royal commission rather than the Law Commission. It has been categorised as social policy rather then lawyers' law reform. This does, however, highlight the vagueness of those terms and indeed a shifting classification system since one would have thought before the Robens Report and the thalidomide debate that this was "lawyers' law." The terms of reference are wide—"to consider to what extent, in what circumstances and by what means compensation should be payable in respect of death or personal injury (including antenatal injury) suffered by any person—

  (a) in the course of employment;
  (b) through the use of a motor vehicle or other means
       of transport;
  (c) through the manufacture, supply or use of goods or
       services;
  (d) on premises belonging to or occupied by another; or
  (e) otherwise through the act or omission of another
       where compensation under the present law is re-
       coverable only on proof of fault or under the rules
       of strict liability, having regard to the cost and other
       implications of the arrangements for the recovery of
       compensation, whether by way of compulsory insur-
       ance or otherwise."

The terms of reference have been cited verbatim to reveal
the scope given to the commission which amounts to no less
than a reappraisal of a large area of the law of tort. The
Law Commission meanwhile has been given the limited
function of ascertaining whether there is a right to recover
compensation in respect of antenatal injuries to assist the
Royal Commission. The reason for this division of labour
appears to be that, as mentioned above, the major task was
regarded as social policy whereas the minor task, one of
"lawyers' law." It should also be added that the Law Commission is represented on the Royal Commission by Mr.
Marsh.

The Law Commission has nonetheless shown a deep concern for the social and economic implications of law in its
Report on Assessment of Damages in Personal Injury Litigation (Law Com. No. 56) by its emphasis on family loss and
preference for official actuarial tables in assessing pecuniary
loss to the irrational system which exists at present.

In criminal law a basic value judgment agreed and acted
upon by the Law Commission[26] is the desirability of establishing a mental element in criminal responsibility. This

necessarily permeates the whole of its proposals for criminal law reform.

In family law above all, as Sir Leslie Scarman has made clear,[27] the law cannot be reformed without making certain judgments as to the requirements of society in a very controversial field. In its work the Law Commission considered the views expressed in and following the Morton Committee and the pamphlet "Putting Asunder: a Divorce law for Contemporary Society" produced by a group set up by the Archbishop of Canterbury, when producing their own Report *Field of Choice*.[28] The Law Commission tried in its Report to discuss what was legally possible leaving the ultimate choice to Parliament. It did, however, as Sir Leslie again made clear, commit itself to two of the most obvious social value judgments. These are set out in paragraph 25. In their view:

"Accordingly, as it seems to us, a good divorce law should seek to achieve the following objectives:

(i) to butress rather than to undermine, the stability of marriage, and

(ii) when regrettably, a marriage has irretrievably broken down, to enable the empty shell to be destroyed with the maximum fairness and the minimum bitterness, distress and humiliation."

In Sir Leslie's view it did not need any exercise of critical judgment on the part of the Commission to commit itself to these value positions. The Report has been criticised[29] and it may be partly with that in mind that the Commission later sought to discover public facts and attitudes by a survey on family property.[30]

The actual survey carried out by the Social Surveys Division of the Office of Population Censuses and Surveys by J. E. Todd and L. M. Jones can be criticised on a number of counts. First there was a sampling deficiency. The method of sampling private addresses and then selecting married and formerly married people did not produce a random sample of married people but merely addresses. Secondly it was the general practice to interview couples together, a method which was likely to lead to bias and answers prompted by the desire to appear reasonable. Thirdly, there was some difficulty in explaining the purpose of the survey which might have affected responses. Lastly the postal strike affected the survey with the result that the response rates of 80 per cent. for married couples and 71 per cent. for formerly married couples were low for a survey of this kind.

The problem that the Law Commissions face identifying and weighing social value judgments in public opinion highlights the complexity of social phenomena and the comparative crudity of social science research methods. The social scientist cannot reduce a section of society to the clinical conditions equivalent to those of the physical scientist. Also there is the problem of numbers and the dangers of selection and interpretation.

The methods used for an exercise such as this are intuition, observation, documentary research and participant/observation case studies, and questionnaires based on random sampling of sections of society.[31] Questionnaires can be of many different types. The most common are the simple yes/no type, multiple choice and the case method type. In addition there are rating and ranking tests, and various variations on the theme of attitude scales. Each of these methods possesses its own types of difficulties and the literature on them is immense. Roscoe Pound in attempting to identify his jural postulates of contemporary American society used the first three methods.[32] Since his time social scientists and statisticians have acquired greater finesse in drafting questionnaires and interpreting their results.[33] Critics of social surveys are quick to emphasise their fallibility but one strong plea in their defence which can be put forward is that the law in operation is accustomed to dealing with less than perfect evidence and this after all forms the fact perimeter of case law. Both the civil and criminal standards of proof allow for imperfections and in the case of opinion polls there is the possibility of actually measuring the degree of uncertainty.

Granted these techniques there nevertheless remains the very basic problem of the low level of cognitive response to questions of values which the Law Commission might pose. The low level of awareness and consistency in mass publics has been emphasised in the political context by a number of writers over the last decade.[34] Certain issues can be simplified and a response obtained. Others, and this might apply to many legal topics, cannot.

Also, even assuming it is possible to identify values within tolerance limits there still remains the problem of resolving conflicts between them. There are in theory in this context two main methods. First a pre-determined scale[35] of which Bentham's attempt at a calculus of felicity is a rather farcical example. The arguments against this are that the scale itself is dependent on a value system and this of course is true; and secondly that social phenomena are too complex to be measured by such a scale. In other words the choice will rarely be a straightforward one anyway. The utilitarian conviction that all values are measurable is merely the resolve to recognise as value only that which is measurable. The second method is that of an *ad hoc* choice and again the main criticism is that the act of choice itself involves a value judgment of preferring one value to another. It seems then that one cannot escape from the slippery ground of values to the surer ground of fact. Now this is true as regards the values themselves but it is possible to a certain extent to quantify the social consequences of preferring one value to another in a particular social context. One will, of course, still be left at the end of the day with preferring one set of circumstances to another and this is a value judgment. Some such ultimate choice is inescapable, and it is not a complete answer for a law reformer to say that the ultimate choice rests with Parliament. In this context it is mainly considering proposals, and choices have to be made in the formulation of the proposals. The important thing is to introduce as much background of social fact and reasoned argument based on fact into the process of law reform as possible. Such work has been done to an increasing degree in criminology in a growing number of centres and in the legal system in general at the Institute of Judicial Administration at Birmingham University. The introduction of social surveys into the research by the Law Commission and the institution of a centre for socio-legal studies at Oxford are to be welcomed. For too long law reform has been carried out on the basis of *a priori* assertions or intuitive assessments of social facts and social consequences by lawyers. In the words of Lord Wilberforce law reform is too serious a matter to be entrusted to the lawyers.[36]

Notes

[1] See the lucid article by Yehezkel Dror "Law and Social Change" in (1959) 33 Tulane L.R. 749. See generally Dicey, *Law and Opinion in the Nineteenth Century.*

[2] See G. C. Moodie and G. Studdert-Kennedy, *Opinion, Publics and Pressure Groups*, pp. 27 *et seq.*

[3] *Op. cit.*, p. 1 and Lecture IV.

[4] See M. Abrams, *Social Surveys and Social Action*, p. 63 and John Madge, *The Tools of Social Science*, pp. 179-180.

[5] See H. Mannheim in *Law and Opinion in England in the Twentieth Century* (ed. M. Ginsberg), pp. 265-66.

[6] Following the *Shorter Oxford Dictionary* definition of opinion and the basic definition adopted by William Albig in *Public Opinion*, p. 1; see also Albig's discussion of "public."

[7] See Albig, *op. cit.*, p. 8.

[8] See F. Znaniecki, *The Method of Sociology*, p. 113.

[9] See generally Moodie and Studdert-Kennedy, *op. cit.*

[10] *Ibid.*, pp. 60 *et seq.*

[11] See S. E. Finer, *The Anonymous Empire*, p. 113; and B. Crick, *In Defence of Politics*, especially Chapter 1.

[12] P.E.P., *Advisory Committees in British Government*, pp. 112-13

[13] See *Principles of Morals and Legislation*, Chap. II, para. XII.

[14] *Op. cit.*, p. 10.

[15] See his speech at Bristol contained in *Edmund Burke—Selections* (ed. A. M. D. Hughes), p. 63.

[16] Law Com. No. 1 and see the stimulating article by Prof. G. Sawer "The Legal Theory of Law Reform" (1970) 20 University of Toronto, L.J. 183, 188.

[17] See "Law in the Consumer Perspective" in *Confronting Injustice* (ed. LL. Cahn), p. 15.

[18] Law Com. No. 24.

[19] *Ibid.*

[20] Law Com. No. 40.

[21] Working Papers No. 32 and 37.

[22] Law Com. No. 9.

[23] Working Paper No. 36.

[24] Law Com. No. 11.

[25] Law Com. No. 32.

[26] Law Com. No. 10 and Working Paper No. 31.

[27] *Law Reform—The New Pattern*, Lecture 2.

[28] Law Com. No. 6. See, however, Leo Abse, *Private Member*, p. 182.

[29] See *e.g.* Michael Freeman, "The Search for a Rational Divorce Law" (1971) 24 C.P.L. 178. See also his excellent article "Towards a Rational Reconstruction of Family Property Law" (1972) 25 C.L.P. 84 for a stimulating jurisprudential discussion of legal change in the field of matrimonial property and a criticism of some of the Law Commission's thinking. The working paper discussed is now a Report (Law Com. No. 52). The Report makes considerable use of the Social Survey results.

[30] "Matrimonial Property" by the Social Surveys Division of the Office of Population Censuses and Surveys and Ruth Deech's article, "A Tide in the Affairs of Women" (1972) 122 New.L.J. 742.

[31] See generally J. Madge, *The Tools of Social Science*.

[32] R. Pound, *Contemporary Juristic Theory*, p. 76.

[33] See the long but excellent article by Walter J. Blum and Harry Kalvern Jr. "The Art of Opinion Research: a lawyer's appraisal of an Emerging Science" (1956) 24 University of Chicago L.R. 1. See also Hans Zeisel "The Uniqueness of Survey Evidence" (1960) 45 Cornell L.Q. 322.

[34] H. L. Deb., Vol. 264, col. 1177.

[35] For a useful attempt to elicit a hierarchy of values from the common law see R. W. M. Dias in "The Value of a Value-study of Law" (1965) 28 M.L.R. 397 and *Jurisprudence* (3rd ed.), Chap. 7. See also F. E. Dowrick, "Lawyers' Values and Law Reform" (1963) 79 L.Q.R. 556.

[36] H. L. Deb., Vol. 264, cols. 1171 *et. seq.*

CHAPTER 7

SOME COMPARISONS

IN this chapter we shall examine law reform on the national level and we shall look first at New Zealand, secondly at the United States of America, and thirdly at France with brief references to Germany.

1. New Zealand

New Zealand is an interesting and useful Commonwealth country to compare with the United Kingdom in the field of law reform, since it has a number of significant similarities and differences.[1]

From its early days as a British colony it has shown a great willingness to use the medium of legislation to make improvements and remedy social ills. Many of the early settlers who went there felt that they had escaped the evils of a social system they condemned and looked forward to a life nearer to their ideals. However, with them and before them were a more hardened and cynical group of mixed origin and sometimes dubious background. There was also sporadic conflict with the Maoris which later developed into war. Life in this early period was hard and often turbulent. The need was felt for an adequate system of administration of justice.[2]

The issue was put bluntly by James Stephen, Under Secretary of the Colonial Office at the time[3]:

"In the infancy of a colony the choice must be made between the adoption of an old and inapplicable code or of a new and immature code. Both are evils but in my mind it is much safer to begin with a vigorous effort to lay the foundations of law on a right and durable basis, than to build it on a basis which must be wrong and which can never possess any stability."

New Zealand was fortunate in having men such as Chief Justice William Martin and Attorney-General William Swainson in its service.[4] Swainson, assisted at times by Martin, had drafted many of the ordinances in the period before representative government. In 1859 he wrote of the early period[5]—"Not being hampered by any complicated pre-existing system, nor impeded by the opposing influence of a powerful profession, the law givers of the colony were enabled to effect amendments in the law which the British legislature has hardly yet succeeded in accomplishing." In 1873 a Ministry of Justice was set up to superintend the administration of justice but it did not play an active role in law reform until later. In the period 1875 to 1910 the New Zealand Parliament showed great willingness to make fundamental reforms in many areas of law. The Hon. Mr. J. R. Hanan, who was Minister of Justice and Attorney-General, in a pamphlet entitled "The Law in a Changing Society" published in 1965 described this period as one in which the New Zealand Parliament did not hesitate to borrow from a wide variety of sources within and even outside the common law world nor on occasion to act as the pioneer of new measures.[6] Many reforms made in New Zealand in this period were not effected in England for another generation or more; some are still not achieved there. "There was the introduction of the land transfer system and of adoption, legitimation by subsequent marriage and family protection. The divorce law was greatly liberalised. Criminal law was codified and improved, a new code of court procedure enacted and a large measure of liability in

tort was imposed on the Crown. This was in addition to a
host of less fundamental improvements and the routine adoption of United Kingdom legislation in commercial law
and in other branches."

After 1910 although law reform continued it had lost its
early momentum and there was some dissatisfaction over
the failure to keep the law up to date and to take advantage
of improvements made in England and abroad. One of the
main problems was that, as in England, law reform was
due primarily to particular enthusiasms of individuals and
there was no permanent machinery to keep the law under
review.

However in 1937 a Law Revision Committee was set up
and the Department of Justice was given specific responsibility for law reform. These, as Mr. Hanan pointed out,
were "most significant steps forward. For the first time there
was an organisation within the framework of government
charged with taking the law in hand to bring and keep it
up to date."[7] The setting up of the committee was influenced
by the creation of the English Law Revision Committee in
1934 and a debate which took place at the Dominion Law
Conference in 1936.[8] Despite the influence of the English
model the New Zealand committee was different in scope
and membership. It had no formal constitution and was
unrestricted in its scope. Its inaugural meeting was attended
on the Minister of Justice's invitation by the Chief Justice,
the Solicitor-General, two representatives appointed by the
New Zealand Law Society, one law teacher, the Under-
Secretary for Justice and the parliamentary law draftsmen.
Later the Chief Justice considered that being a judge he ought
not to take part in the committee's actual discussions although he offered his services in an advisory capacity.[9] By
1965 the committee had grown and comprised four representatives of the New Zealand Law Society, one law teacher
from each of the universities teaching law, a nominee of
the parliamentary Opposition, the Chairman of the Statute

Law Revision Committee, a lawyer who was formerly an M.P., another lawyer who was a former law teacher representative, the Solicitor-General, the law draftsman and the Secretary for Justice. The Minister of Justice has always been Chairman and the Department of Justice which provides the secretariat was and is the co-ordinating authority for marshalling matters to be considered and for superintending the presentation of the proposals for legislative action.

As in the case of the English Law Revision Committee progress was impeded by the war. After that, Mr. Hanan in his pamphlet stated that further progress was inhibited by the acute shortage of qualified staff. "There was a lack of appreciation, apart from those immediately concerned, of the importance of full research and the need to attract and hold persons of high calibre. The truth is that a comprehensive policy of law reform was attempted on a shoe string."[10]

Another cause to which Mr. Hanan referred was a general unwillingness to consider significant changes in the common law except in the wake of English legislation. This was particularly true in the traditional areas of judge-made law where it acted as a brake on progress aggravated by the comparative lack of action in England itself. Coupled with this was a neglect of the experience of other countries which, as we have seen, was certainly not the case in the last part of the nineteenth century.

However, despite Mr. Hanan's dissatisfaction, the record of New Zealand during these two decades was quite impressive. Amongst the more outstanding reforms of this period were the introduction of an Ombudsman, a review of the entire criminal code and law of procedure (other than the civil procedure of the High Court), the introduction of compensation for criminal injuries, reforms in family law, the law of real property, charitable trusts, and various aspects of the law of torts. Two other radical reforms which might be mentioned because they illustrate that Mr. Hanan's implication that New Zealand was tied to the mother country's apronstrings must be read with qualification are the abolition of the rule that money paid under a mistake of law cannot generally be recovered and the creation of a remedy where services are rendered in return for an unfulfilled promise to make provision in a will. Both are extremely useful reforms which could well be introduced into English Law.

In 1965 partly as a result of the proposals in the United Kingdom to create Law Commissions and partly it seems as a result of a Students' Conference on Law Reform in Auckland in April 1965, Mr. Hanan reconsidered the existing machinery for reform and made some proposals for its re-organisation.

Let us first look at the machinery as it existed in 1965. Unlike the archaic and extraordinary division of labours of the English system which gives to the Lord Chancellor an ill-defined responsibility for reform which he shares primarily with the Home Secretary and Department of Trade and Industry the New Zealand system is relatively straight-forward. First there is the Minister of Justice who is responsible to Parliament for the state of law. Since 1935 he has always been the same person holding the office of Attorney-General. He is assisted by the Law Drafting Office and the Department of Justice. The Law Drafting Office not only drafts the Bills but also plays some part in discussing matters of priority which arise in the drafting of them.

The function of the Department of Justice in relation to law reform[11] are—

1. To advise the Minister on formation of policy and on policy aspects of reforms.
2. To initiate reform proposals and refer them to the permanent law reform committees or to *ad hoc* committees.
3. To find a place for reform proposals acceptable to the Minister and the government in the legislative programme.

4. To co-operate with the law draftsman.
5. To assist the Minister and parliamentary committee during the progress of Bills before the House.

The Ministry of Justice suffers from high staff turnover and this plus its other legal work cuts down its effectiveness to some extent.[12]

As we have seen from 1937 the Department of Justice was assisted by the Law Revision Committee. The Committee usually met twice a year to consider proposals. Its members were unpaid (except for reimbursement of travelling expenses). Mr. Hanan thought this was wrong.

In addition to the Law Revision Committee there was the Rules Committee and the Company Law Advisory Committee.

Mr. Hanan drew attention to certain advantages of the New Zealand machinery. First, the existence of a permanent Department of Justice ensures that law reform recommendations are, (subject to the Minister's approval) placed on the legislation programme at the beginning of each year and as high a priority given to them as is reasonable. The members of the department work closely with the law draftsman on the preparation of a Bill. Secondly, a simple and effective Parliamentary procedure has been evolved to deal with small and non-conscientious changes. This is the Statutes Amendment Bill which is introduced as a single Bill and separated into a number of individual Bills during the committee stage.

Lastly, a point which he did not make but which needs to be emphasised about New Zealand is that Parliament has been uni-cameral since 1950 when the Legislative Council, an appointive body, was abolished. Legislation is thus an easier process than in the United Kingdom.

Having surveyed the existing machinery in 1965 Mr. Hanan considered law reform abroad[13] and came to the conclusion that the New York system (which will be considered later) was nearer to the New Zealand system than the latter was to the English system pre-1965.[14] He considered whether the Law Commission proposals should be adopted in New Zealand and came to the conclusion that they should not.[15] His reasons were primarily that the differences between the two systems rendered it inappropriate. In New Zealand the preparation of almost all legislation was done by the government. Law reform was no exception. "To some degree almost every substantial measure is a policy measure, however divorced it may be from party politics in the ordinary sense."[16]

Thus the execution of a programme of law reform must be the responsibility of the government through the Minister of Justice. The creation of an English-style Law Commission would duplicate the existing machinery outlined above. Further, by taking the work further away from the normal constitutional agencies it might actually impede reform. "Too much stress cannot be laid on the fact that much of the comparative success of law reform in New Zealand is owed to the presence on our Law Revision Committee of the Minister of Justice as Chairman and of a representative of the Opposition. Nor is it desirable that the staff engaged in research into and examination of proposals should be divorced from ordinary contact with practical administration and the public or from direct recourse to the specialists available to a department."[16]

Thirdly,[17] the need for consolidation and statute law revision was not as much a problem in New Zealand where most of the legislation in force was post-1908. Also the New Zealanders had adopted the practice of textual amendment.

The solution to New Zealand's problems lay in being more outward looking and not depending on the United Kingdom as the source of outside ideas. "The primary aim should be to select whatever seems best for New Zealand and freely adapt it to our needs and desires, whether it comes from England or another country or is an original product."[10] New Zealand should look to Scotland, the United States and

Scandinavia as other sources of ideas. As Mr. Hanan put it "No protective duties or shortage of exchange impairs the unrestricted import of ideas ..."[19]

Despite the decision not to follow the English pattern it was decided to effect some reorganisation.[20] An attempt was to be made to strengthen and expand the Law Drafting Office and the Ministry of Justice, in particular to recruit more good staff.

The Law Revision Committee was to be reconstituted as a Law Revision Commission of twelve or so members appointed by and under the chairmanship of the Minister to supervise the law reform programme. It was to be this Commission's job to "map out the territory, to decide priorities, to allocate particular items to standing committees, special committees or other bodies and to review progress annually."[21] In this respect the New Zealand Commission has things in common with the Law Commissions.

In addition to the Law Revision Commission there were to be a number of standing committees covering various parts of the law to which proposals were to be referred. These could request reports from sub-committees and government departments. The standing committees would make reports direct to the Minister.

Also there would still be a need for special committees to consider some areas particularly where "the need for obtaining information and views of interested sections by means of formal submissions looms large."[22] These again would report to the Minister. The judiciary might be more actively involved in law reform in this way.

All the non-civil servant members of these committees should be paid. Further, special studies and research papers should be commissioned and if necessary a further law review subsidised.

What progress has there been to date? In 1966 the Law Revision Commission and four (later five) standing committees were set up of about eight members, each responsible for a particular area of law. Thus there are now the Contracts and Commercial Law Reform Committee, the Property Law and Equity Reform Committee, the Public and Administrative Law Reform Committee, the Criminal Law Reform Committee and the Tort and General Law Reform Committee.

As before the Law Revision Commission Chairman is the Minister of Justice and there are representatives of the practising legal profession, the law faculties and the legal departments of state. In the first report to Parliament in respect of the year ended March 31, 1971[23] the Commission stated that "as a matter of deliberate policy and in the interests of greater flexibility" its functions had nowhere been precisely defined. In essence it is an advisory body to the Minister. It saw its responsibilities as preparing and overseeing programmes of law reform, reviewing progress, allocating new topics to a standing or special committee and generally advising the government on matters pertaining to law reform policies and programmes. In addition the Commission has taken a direct interest itself in certain topics.

Ruth Deech in an article entitled "Law Reform: The Choice of Method"[24] has criticised Mr. Hanan's reorganisation on two counts. First the comparative informality of the system means that its existence is "comparatively precarious, at least in theory." It would seem that with the traditional keenness for reform that the New Zealanders have shown this is not a point to be taken seriously. After all the new machinery in England is considerably under the control of the Lord Chancellor of the day. A second and more telling criticism is that the new system of Commission and committees with the latter reporting direct to the Minister and not to the Commission which handed down a particular topic in the first place is "expensive and cumbersome." There does appear to have been an excessive desire for control by the Minister. However, this point is mitigated to some exent by the practice of appointing as chairman of the committees members of the Commission. Also no report of a committee carries the Commission's authority until approved at a meeting of the Commission. The delegation of functions seems on the whole sensible in view of the fact that law reform is still very much a part time activity of many of the members of the Commissions and committees.

As at March 31, 1972 there were also in existence *ad hoc* committees on Shipping, Company Law and Matrimonial Property.

The wisdom of the flexibility of the New Zealand system in fact has been borne out to some degree in the English practice of retaining two of the existing law reform committees in existence and the delegation of further tasks by the government to *ad hoc* committees with a broader base.

One last feature of the New Zealand system on which we will comment is the development of co-operation with Australia over the last decade in particular though the medium of the meetings of the Australian and New Zealand Law Ministers. Particular interest is being shown in the Australian work on company law reform, securities legislation and consumer credit where Australia is more advanced than New Zealand. Formal arrangements have been made with the State of Western Australia to maintain a register of law reform projects in Australia and New Zealand and for a system of pooling of information. This will help to supplement the rather limited resources that New Zealand can make available for research.[25]

2. The United States of America

In the United States law reform is carried out at two stages, the federal and the state. At the federal level the main aim is harmonisation. The desirability of uniformity in at least part of the laws of the various jurisdictions has long been recognised. This received recognition at the time of the formation of the American Bar Association in 1878 by the inclusion of a statement in the constitution that one of its objects was "to promote ... uniformity of legislation throughout the nation." As a result of initiative by the Alabama Bar Association land the American Bar Association there has been in existence since 1892 the National Conference of Commissioners on Uniform State Laws.[26] The Conference is composed of commissioners (usually three in number) appointed by the governors of each state normally for five-year terms. In addition to the commissioners there are past commissioners who have served for twenty years who are usually elected to life membership. Also the principal administrative officers of each state legislative reference bureau or other agency charged by law with the drafting of legislation are *ex officio* associate members of the Conference. As such the latter have the privileges of the floor, are eligible to serve on committees but do not have the right to vote in the Conference.

The Conference is formally organised under a constitution and by-laws. The Conference meets annually for a convention of six days at which it considers legislation drafted by subcommittees. This convenes at the site of the American Bar Association's annual meeting, which it precedes.

The Conference maintains its headquarters office and a permanent staff in the American Bar Centre in Chicago. Much of its preliminary work is done there and elsewhere between annual meetings by individuals and by sub-committees through correspondence and in special meetings. For each contemplated piece of legislation the president appoints a special committee to investigate and, if deemed desirable, draft the Act. In the case of the more important Acts, an expert draftsman is sometimes employed to work with the committee. During the preparation the committee liaises with the relevant committee of the American Bar Association and in appropriate cases with officers of the Council of State Governments and the Interstate Commission on Crime, with representatives of industry, finance, labour and with other individuals conversant in the field.

The draft is then submitted to a section of the Conference (*i.e.* another committee). Often extensive revision is made at this meeting. The draft is referred to the Conference Committee on Style and then circulated to the Conference at large. At both the section and Conference meetings outsiders are sometimes invited to speak.

Sometimes a particular Act is considered over a number of conferences. Ultimately after at least two conferences the Act receives the final approval of the Conference and the section of the House of Delegates of the American Bar Association and is then recommended to the various jurisdictions for adoption.

The legislation falls into two categories—uniform and model Acts. Uniform Acts are promulgated in areas of law where the Conference feels that uniformity among the jurisdictions is desirable. Model Acts are drafted for areas of law where although there is no pressing need for uniformity, there seems to be a demand for legislation in a substantial number of states. Uniform Acts are recommended for all jurisdictions to adopt. Model Acts are prepared merely for the convenience of such legislative bodies as may be interested. Opinions often differ as how a particular Act should be classified. Where the division of opinion is close the Conference tends to designate the Act as a uniform Act.

Uniform Acts passed by the state legislatures are given short titles labelling them as Uniform Acts and since 1912 it has been the general practice to insert a provision that the Act shall be "so interpreted as to effectuate its purpose to make uniform" the law of those states or jurisdictions adopting it.[27]

The main defects of this institution are sometimes said to be first that the work is voluntary and unpaid or if remunerated by the states badly remunerated and secondly the number of subjects in which national conformity is essential is limited. The principal achievement which was undertaken in conjunction with the American Law Institute has been the

Uniform Commercial Code which was proposed as a uniform Act and has now been generally adopted in the various states although sometimes with modifications.[28]

The American Law Institute had its origins in a project for a "juristic center for the betterment of law" which was proposed by members of the Association of American Law Schools and was established in 1923.[29] Its constitution declares its objects are "to promote the clarification and simplification of the law and its better adaptation to social needs, and to encourage and carry on scholarly and scientific legal work."[30]

In the report of the committee which recommended its establishment it was argued that the need arose because of uncertainty and complexity in the law, exacerbated by the varying standards of legal text books and the fact that they were not generally critical or constructive.[31] The writers' approach tended to be that of a photographer. One principal reason for this was the great volume of case law.

A first priority should be to reduce the uncertainty and complexity and this should be achieved by means of a series of "restatements" of the law.

The character of the restatement[32] they had in mind could best be described as at once analytical, critical and constructive. Analytical in the sense of a division of topics based on a definite classification system, each in its turn being treated analytically rather than historically. Critical in the sense that the reason for the law as it is should be set forth or where it is uncertain the reasons in support of each suggested solution should be carefully considered. Constructive in the sense that it should take account of situations not yet discussed by courts or dealt with by legislatures but which are likely to cause litigation in the future. Again where the law was uncertain or there were differing views in the different jurisdictions the restatement should choose the "proper rule of law." The committee then considered what should be included and excluded and made some useful comments which are relevant to all law reform; they maintained that "changes in the law which are, or would, if proposed, become a matter of general public concern and discussion should not be considered, much less set forth in any restatement of law which" they had in mind. However, reforms which carried out efficiently ends that were generally accepted as desirable were to be within the restatement's function. Also, when a topic had become generally accepted as no longer a subject for public controversy then it could be included.

The changes proposed would then be either in the direction of simplifying the law where it is unnecessarily complex or in the direction of the better adaptation of the details of the law to the accomplishment of ends generally considered to be desirable.

The actual method[33] recommended by the committee and used by the Institute is as follows. First it determines that a restatement of the law on a given topic should be made, then the work is entrusted to members of committee who are selected for their specialist knowledge. Reporters are selected who are primarily responsible for the first draft which is then circulated for comments. The final draft is then submitted to the Council and to members before final adoption. Membership of the Council, the committees and of the Institute itself is drawn from the Bench, the Bar and academic lawyers.

The form[34] of the restatement was discussed in the committee's report and their comments are of interest particularly since the Law Commission's reports have tended in some respects to follow it and it has been suggested that their statement of principles is the form that the codes being produced by the Law Commission might take.

First there should be a separation of the statement of legal principle from the analysis of the legal problems involved, the statement of the present condition of the law and the reasons in support of the principles.

The statement of principles should follow the form of a

well drawn statute. This necessity for precise statement would tend to make the writers give careful examination of the effect of the proposed change in the light of other provisions of the restatement. The statement of principles should be much more complete than that found in civil law codes, since this is the present characteristic of the common law. Then there should be a thorough discussion of legal theory together with a careful examination of the present law.

Those who are familiar with some of the restatements will realise that despite this, particular restatements differ in content, quality and style. The idea of publishing accompanying treatises was dropped. Such works could not be written by committees. The restatement thus speaks *ex cathedra*.

The restatements are, as Professor Twining has recently pointed out, theoretical hybrids glossing over the difference between description and prescription of the law.

Their value has been their accessibility, simplicity and decisiveness. Their weakness has been their excessive caution and their predominantly legalistic outlook.

Why was this particular method adopted? Twining argues that there were three main factors. First, state legislatures should be by-passed. Secondly, America was drowning in a sea of precedents of persuasive authority. Thirdly, the restatements would generate their own authority and influence. These would depend on the extent to which they were used by Bar and Bench. This meant that Utopian schemes were out.

Lastly, we must consider the principal differences between the Institute and the Law Commissions. The American Law Institute, unlike the Law Commission, is the product of the law teachers, organised by them and the profession and funded by the profession and from charitable rather than government funds. Its particular role and peculiar method have been and are necessitated by the political geography of the United States.

The position of the judiciary has perhaps been weakened by the creation of the American Law Institute. On the other hand, academics engaged in the work of the Institute hold a position comparable to the civilian law teacher writing doctrine.[35]

The role of the restatements, however, was not necessarily to provide the blue print for a code.[36] The United States had perhaps been more active in practical codification in the nineteenth century than the United Kingdom. Dudley Field,[37] inspired by Bentham's writings, had produced codes on differing topics some of which were adopted by states of the union but which were principally successful in the pioneering west. Louisiana had inherited a civil law tradition. Nevertheless these experiences had tended to make the American legal profession on the whole sceptical on the question of codes. The committee's report to which reference has been made emphasised that their role was not codification but to maintain and resuscitate the common law which possessed the advantages of flexibility and fullness of detail. They feared the rigidity which would set in if the results were reduced to statute form and the danger of injustice resulting from unforeseen facts. On the other hand they did not reject altogether the interesting suggestion[38] which had been put forward that the restatements might be adopted by state legislatures with the proviso that they should have the force of principles enunciated as the basis of decisions of the highest court of the state, the courts having power to declare modifications and exceptions. Such action would at once give an authority to the restatement which it would otherwise not possess and at the same time would not fetter the courts as would a formal code. Also the courts would have greater freedom in adopting the rules laid down in the restatement and at the same time be free to deal with those cases which would inevitably arise where the rigid application of the principles set forth in the restatement would result in injustice. It would seem that here is one lesson from abroad which the Law Commissions might learn. We shall return to this in Chapter 9.

Further useful comparisons can be made at state level. At the state level there are numerous law reform committees prominent amongst which are the New York Law Revision Commission[39] set up in 1934 and the Louisiana Law Institute set up in 1938. Most of these have adopted as their main object that of the American Law Institute cited above. Others follow that of the New York Law Revision Commission which was set up at the same time as the English Law Revision Committee. Its objects were wider, however, than the rather limited terms of reference given to that body and in some respects are wider than those stated in the Law Commissions Act 1965. They are:

"1. To examine the common law and statutes of the state and current judicial decisions for the purpose of discovering defects and anachronisms in the law and recommending needed reforms.

2. To receive and consider proposed changes in the law recommended by the American Law Institute, the commissioners for the promotion of uniformity of legislation in the United States, any bar association or other learned bodies.

3. To receive and consider suggestions from judges, justices, public officials, lawyers and the public generally as to defects and anachronisms in the law.

4. To recommend, from time to time, such changes in the law as it deems necessary to modify or eliminate antiquated and inequitable rules of law, and to bring the law of this state, civil and criminal, into harmony with modern conditions."

The New York Commission according to its report for 1972[40] has recently undertaken a number of studies at the direction of the legislature, the Governor, members of the judiciary, the Bar and laymen. Its procedures are similar to the Law Commission. Indeed it would seem that some of the English procedures were borrowed from it, in particular the practices of widespread consultation, internal drafting of bills and liaison with the legislature. One important difference, however, is that like the New Zealand system the introduction of proposals into the legislature is commonly arranged by the *ex officio* members of the Commission.

3. France and Germany

Turning to the Civil Law jurisdictions, both France and Germany operate with Ministries of Justice under which are specialist committees dealing with various areas of law and the legal system.[41] France also has a *Conseil d'Etat*[42] which in its present basic form was a product of the Revolution of 1789 and plays a key role in government. A civil service body, it performs a consultative as well as a judicial role. All Bills introduced into Parliament have to be submitted to the *Conseil* for its advice. The advice once given need not necessarily be followed—at least in fact if not in theory. The government can ignore it and there is no further sanction. The *Conseil*'s advice is normally given by the general assembly of the *Conseil* after a report from the relevant section of the *Conseil*. Where the matter is more urgent the general assembly can be replaced by a smaller standing committee. Since reforms in 1963 the *Conseil* also has the duty of submitting an annual report to the President which deals *inter alia* with what legal or administrative reforms it considers desirable. These reports are not required to be published. As can be seen from these brief references the *Conseil d'Etat* performs a much more active and influential role in government than the Law Commission.

From the point of view of comparison, however, it is perhaps more useful to look briefly at the past and at the contrasting methods used by France and Germany in their codification projects.

The French Civil Code was of course the first of the modern codes although Frederick the Great had commissioned and brought into force the *Allgemeine Landrecht für die Preussischen Staaten* in 1794.[43] Various attempts had been made during the early days of the French Revolution to produce a code but these had failed. The matter was taken up by Napoleon as first consul in 1800. He[44] appointed a commission of four (Tronchet, President of the *Cour de Cassation*, Bigot du Preameneu, Government Commissioner, Portalis, Government Commissioner and Malleville, judge of the *Cour de Cassation*) to prepare a draft.

They divided the work amongst themselves and handed in a draft within four months. It was submitted to the courts for suggestions. There was opposition in the legislature where the draft was attacked as a servile copy of Roman law and the old *droit coutumier*. However, Napoleon in a *coup d'état* reformed the legislature, reducing it to fifty members on whose support he could count.

The resulting code was passed in thirty-six statutes in 1803 united in the *Code Civil des Français* in March 1804, comprising 2281 articles.

By an express provision in the code, Roman law, the ordinances, customs and earlier legislation ceased to have effect with regard to matters covered by the code.

By contrast the German Civil Code[45] was a product of the late nineteenth century. The first commission was appointed in 1874 consisting of six judges, three practising lawyers and two law professors. They divided up the work and drafts were produced for all sections in 1880. From 1880 to 1887 all the commissioners examined the whole and the draft code was then published in 1887 and criticism invited. As Roscoe Pound has stated "The whole and every part was subjected to searching criticism by everybody—lawyers, publicists, businessmen, clergymen and labor leaders." After three years all the criticisms were collated and published and in 1890 a new commission was set up, consisting of eight judges, two practising lawyers and one professor to draw up the code *de novo* with the first draft and the criticisms as a brief. It took six years. It was published in 1896 and enacted and took effect in 1900.

It is, however, not only from the methods but the aims that we can draw useful comparisons. The French code did not aim at anything grand from a philosophical point of view. Its draftsmen had no wish to bind posterity.[46] "They were more concerned to sum up the teaching of the past in compendious and accessible form and to settle controversies which had already arisen or were likely to arise in the future."[47] They left gaps which could only be filled by methods similar to those of common law. The Germans on the other hand aimed at a complete statement of law by means of interlocking concepts, principles and rules. The aim was to enable the practitioner to find a complete answer by using the code.[48]

From the beginning in France there have been piecemeal amendments and reform and in recent times work on fundamental revision of the codes. The idea of revision of the *Code Civil*, however, is not new. Napoleon in a letter to Prince de Bénévent realised that its imperfections would be revealed by experience.[49]

In the nineteenth century the major revisions took place in the other European countries such as Germany which had based or were proposing to base their law upon the *Code Civil*. In France as early as 1837 some dissatisfaction was being expressed by an eminent jurist. Later in 1865-66 Batbie and Duverger in articles in the *Revue Critique de Legislation* called for a revision of the code in certain respects; Acollas called for more sweeping reforms in 1866. On the commencement in operation of the German Code and the centenary of the *Code Civil*, there was a division of opinion amongst eminent jurists in the *Livre du Centenaire*, Larnaude and Pilon being for and Planiol and Gaudemet against revision. The Minister of Justice appointed a commission to prepare a preliminary draft but this was too large and did not finish its work.[50]

In the inter-war years there was some further call for revision on the annexation of Alsace–Lorraine.

The real initiative, however, came on the morrow of the liberation of France in 1945 when, after pressure from the *Association Henri Capitant*, the Minister of Justice of the provisional government set up a commission with the task of a general reform of the *Code Civil*. Later in 1947 another commission was set up to reform the *Code de Commerce* and the Law of Companies. Further commissions were set up for other areas of law later.[51]

It is interesting to note that the French followed their own precedents of having a committee instead of delegating the task to a single individual. This is in contrast with the earlier examples of the Netherlands, Chile and Switzerland where such tasks had been delegated to a single jurist. The risk as Professor Juillot de la Morandière, president of the commission, recognised is that of less unity in the work but the risks avoided are obviously much greater, as the English Law Commission has learnt in its work on codification.

The commission appointed, although larger than that of 1804, was much smaller than the abortive commission of 1900 which had consisted not only of lawyers, jurists and the bench but also parliamentarians, businessmen and writers. The commission set up in 1945 consisted of twelve members—three professors of law, three *conseillers d'état*, three judges and three practitioners consisting of two *avocats* and one *notaire*. In addition a staff was set up including two judges and one *avocat* with a law professor as head.

The working methods of the commission varied. Originally members of the commission were divided into four sub-committees—general, persons and family, obligations and property. Tentative drafts were prepared and reports presented by members of the sub-commission, a staff member or an outside specialist or civil servant. Texts, when adopted, were then referred to the full commission which endeavoured to meet every two weeks.

Eventually it was found that this system was not working well. The members were too busy and it involved duplication of labours. As Juillot de la Morandière explained[52] "The method proved too slow. The texts which the sub-commission had adopted after numerous meetings were discussed all over again; they were subjected to terse, critical examination by the full commission which often rejected them and sent them back to the sub-committee for a new study. We realised that we would never get anywhere that way and ... we did away with the sub-committees, whose meetings a certain number of members were too busy to attend anymore. It was decided that the preliminary drafts prepared by our secretariat and one of our members would be submitted to the full Commission. The rhythm of production accelerated."

The commission stopped work eleven years ago after presenting to the *Garde des Sceaux* three books containing an avant-projet of the *Code Civil* and M. le Doyen Juillot de la Morandière is now dead.

The preliminary volume of the avant-project deals with the binding force of statutes, administrative acts and diplomatic treaties, and conflicts of law. Volume 1 deals with physical persons and the family and Volume 2 with succession and gifts.

Since then a revision of the Code has been undertaken taking into account the work of the commission.

A special commission acting under the auspices of the Ministry of Justice has considered the problem of adoption and its work led to the law of July 11, 1966. In addition the Government charged one man, M. le Doyen Carbonnier, Professor of Law in the University of Paris, with the responsibility of drawing up proposals for other modifications to the *Code Civil*. As a result the following statutes have been passed:

Law of December 14, 1964 which deals with guardianship of infants;

Law of July 13, 1965 which deals with matrimonial property;

Law of January 3, 1968 on the protection of incapacitated persons;

Law of January 4, 1970 dealing with parental authority;

Law of January 3, 1972 on paternity.

To these can be added two other statutes of great practical importance:

Law of July 3, 1971 on the rules of inheritance;

Law of January 2, 1973 on recovery of maintenance.

Parallel to these reforms of the substantive law a review of procedure has been carried by a commission provided over by M. Jean Foyer, former *Garde des Sceaux* and present President of the *Commission des Lois* of the National Assembly. One of its special objects was to redefine the role of the judge in the conduct of civil litigation. With this in view three important decrees and a statute were brought into force on September 16, 1972 and January 1, 1973 (the decrees of September 9, 1971, July 20, 1972 and August 28, 1972 and the law of July 5, 1972). These constitute the first part of an overhaul of the rules of civil procedure.[53]

Important reforms have also taken place in commercial law especially in the fields of company law and bankruptcy.[54]

Thus France has been and is accomplishing a considerable measure of reform and is clearly experimenting with institutions of law reform and not tying itself down to one particular form.

Without constant revision, as Professor Houin has pointed out[55] the codes cannot continue to fulfil their function either as regards the substance or the form of law. Bentham recognised this in the nineteenth century. Fortunately modern French lawyers have now recognised this and accept that the original codes are no longer sacred and immutable texts.

What general lessons might be learned from these super-ficial comparisons? First that although the Law Commission has apparently borrowed much from American experience it could perhaps learn even more from a reconsideration of the original report of the Committee on the American Law Institute as regards the form of its work and its relationship with the courts and the legislature. The experience of New Zealand and the New York Law Revision Commission highlights the utility of a Ministry of Justice or at least of an established and organised entrée into the legislature. From Europe we can perhaps learn not only that a code needs to be kept up to date (which seems to be common ground between the advocates and opponents of codification) but more fundamentally that an early decision as to the type of code or codes required is needed and that this determines quite substantially the methods to be employed. Perhaps one last important conclusion one can draw from overseas ex-perience with the drafting of codes is that there is no *single* paradigm of a code and that differing forms and styles might be required because of differing legal traditions and might in fact in any case be necessary for different areas of law within the same legal system. Even within particular branches of law there may be areas where there is a need for certainty and other areas where there is a need for flexibility.[56]

Notes

[1] See generally Vol. 4 of *The British Commonwealth—the dev-elopment of its laws and constitutions* (2nd ed. Dr. J. L. Robson, Secretary for Justice of New Zealand) (hereinafter referred to as "B.C.4") and *The Law in a Changing Society—a policy and pro-gramme for law reform* by the Hon. J. R. Hanan, Minister of Justice (hereinafter referred to as "Hanan"). Much of what follows is based on these two works. See also Hamish Gray, "A Rationale of Law Reform" (1966) 2 N.Z.U.L.R. 162; Sir Alexander Kingcombe Turner, "Changing the Law" (1969) 3 N.Z.U.L.R. 404 for some judicial scepticism about "young men in a hurry" in the academic world and a report by D. R. Harris in (1970) 4 N.Z.U.L.R. 45.

[2] See B.C.4 pp. 22 *et seq.* See also J. Hight and H. D. Bamford

The Constitutional History and Law of New Zealand (1914), Part I.

[3] Minute on Governor's Dispatch of March 29, 1842 cited in B.C. 4 at p. 362.

[4] See P. A. Cornford, "The Administration of Justice in New Zealand 1841-1846—(A Legislative Chronicle) Part I" (1970) 4 N.Z.U.L.R. 18 especially at pp. 33-34.

[5] *New Zealand and its Colonisation*, p. 94, cited in B.C.4 at p. 362.

[6] Hanan, p. 5.

[7] *Ibid.*

[8] Hanan, p. 6.

[9] B.C.4, p. 493.

[10] Hanan, p. 6.

[11] Hanan, p. 9.

[12] Hanan, p. 10.

[13] Hanan, pp. 13-17.

[14] Hanan, p. 16.

[15] Hanan, pp. 18-19.

[16] Hanan, p. 18.

[17] Hanan, p. 19.

[18] Hanan, p. 20.

[19] Hanan, p. 29.

[20] Hanan, pp. 22-25.

[21] Hanan, p. 23.

[22] Hanan, p. 24.

[23] Report of the Law Revision Commission for the year ended March 31, 1971, N.Z.H. 20C.

[24] (1969) 47 C.B.R. at pp. 405-409.

[25] 1971 Report, p. 5.

[26] See the Handbooks of the National Conferences of Commissioners on Uniform State Laws and James W. Day, "The National Conference of Commissioners on Uniform State Laws" (1955) 8 University of Florida L.R. 276. See also the comment by W. L. Twining in *Karl Llewellyn and the Realist Movement*, pp. 272 *et seq.*

[27] See Day, *op. cit.*, for the Conference's achievements up to 1955.

[28] See R. Pound, *Jurisprudence*, Vol. 3, p. 721.

[29] See Report of the Committee on the Establishment of a Permanent Organisation for the Improvement of Law, proposing an American Law Institute in *Proceedings of the American Law Institute*, 1, pp. 1-109; William Draper Lewis, *History of the American Law Institute and the First Restatement of the Law—How one did it*; again see Twining, *op. cit.*, pp. 273 *et seq.*

[30] *Ibid.*, p. 41.

[31] *Ibid.*, pp. 7 *et seq.*

[32] *Ibid.*, p. 19.

[33] *Ibid.*, p. 48.

[34] *Ibid.*, p. 19.

[35] See Mitchell Franklin in (1934) 47 H.L.R. 1367, 1371.

[36] *Ibid.*, pp. 23-26. See further Herbert F. Goodrich "Restatement and Codification" in *David Dudley Field, Centenary Essays* (ed. A. Reppy), pp. 241-250.

[37] See Pound, *op. cit.*, pp. 709 *et seq.*

[38] The Report, p. 24. See the ideas expressed by Harlan F. Stone in "Some Aspects of the Problem of Law Simplification" (1923) 23 Col. L.R. 319, 334-337.

[39] See generally John W. MacDonald, "The New York Law Revision Commission" (1965) 28 M.L.R. 1.

[40] State of New York Legislative Document (1972) No. 65.

[41] See the discussion in Andrew Martin Q.C.'s inaugural lecture at the University of Southampton, "Methods of Law Reform" (1967).

[42] See generally L. Neville Brown and J. F. Garner, *French Administrative Law* (2nd ed.) pp. 31-35 and C. J. Hamson "Le Conseil d'Etat Statuant au Contentieux" (1952) 68 L.Q.R. 60 especially pp. 68 *et seq.*

[43] See R. Pound, *op. cit.*, pp. 690 *et seq.*

[44] This section is based on Pound, *op. cit.*, pp. 692 *et seq.*

[45] See Pound, *op. cit.*, 698-99.

[46] See Portalis, *Discours, rapports et travaux inédits sur le code civil*, pp. 7-8.

[47] F. H. Lawson, *A Common Lawyer looks at the Civil Law*, p. 54.

[48] Lawson, *op. cit.*, p. 53.

[49] Cited in Juillot de la Morandière, "The Reform of the French Civil Code" (1948) 97 U. Pa. L.R. 1, 2.

[50] *Ibid.*, pp. 2-7.

[51] See also Roger Houin "Reform of the French Civil Code and the Code of Commerce" (1955) 4 Am. J. Comp. Law 485.

[52] "Preliminary Report on the Civil Code Reform Commission of France" (1955) 16 La. L. Rev. 1, 16-17.

[53] I am grateful to M. le Sous Directeur des Affaires Civiles et du Sceau for the up-to-date information.

[54] For the company law reforms see R. R. Pennington, *Companies in the Common Market* (2nd ed.), Chap. 2. For the bankruptcy reforms see J. H. Farrar, "The EEC Draft Convention on Bankruptcy" [1972] J.B.L. 256, 257 and Goré, "The Administrative Autonomy of Creditors and French Legislation on Bankruptcy" (1969) 17 Am. J. of Comp. L. 5.

[55] Houin, *op. cit.*, pp. 487 *et seq.*

[56] I am indebted to Professor Geoffrey Sawer for making this point to me. See his arguments in the context of criminal law in "The Criminal Law Cannot Stand Still" (1972) Aust. & N.Z. Journal of Criminology 5, 3, p. 137.

Chapter 8

LAW REFORM IN THE INTERNATIONAL FIELD

In the last chapter we made some comparisons between the law reform institutions and methods at the national level. Law reform at the intra-governmental or international level involves two essentially distinct issues:

(a) the unification, harmonisation or rationalisation of municipal legal orders; and

(b) the clarification and development of the international legal order.

Although as the following analysis will show, these two issues pose distinct legal problems of their own, at the practical level the two are often interwoven. To a body such as the Inter-governmental Maritime Consultative Organization it is of equal importance in dealing, say, with oil pollution that international law should define clearly the rights of states to exercise jurisdiction over tankers of their own and of other states' fleets, as it is to clarify and harmonise the ways in which states exercise such jurisdiction as they can claim. Similarly, to mention another contemporary international problem, both legal orders have to be resorted to in providing a solution to hijacking of aeroplanes. As these two examples show in practice it may also be the same organisation which seeks revision of both international and domestic rules on such matters.

Nevertheless the two issues are distinct. The question of

reform of municipal laws of international significance is prominent in the diplomatic activities of many nations at the present time and is being handled by a multiplicity of bodies.

Thus, the United Nations Commission on the International Trade Law ("UNCITRAL") is tackling "the progressive harmonisation and unification of the law of international trade"[1] at the world level.

On a regional basis, the sub-committees of the Council of Europe (of which the United Kingdom is a member), have in the past two decades negotiated more than seventy treaties which are available for signature by its members. Many of these are designed to harmonise the laws of the Member States. While the most well known of the conventions are the Convention for Protection of Human Rights and the Social Charter, the Council has also been the forum for discussion of harmonisation and reform on such diverse topics as multiple nationality, patents, registration of wills and au pair placements.[2] One of the specialist groups of the Council is the Conference of European Ministers of Justice which has become a regular biennial event and "which plays an important part in directing the legal programme of the Council of Europe."[3]

Even more significant to the United Kingdom and the other Member States at the present time is the work of the European Communities. The European Economic Community is interesting from the point of view of law reform because it is a new species of supra-national authority existing primarily for economic purposes with its basic values or "operative ideals," as Pound might have described them, clearly set out in a series of principles enunciated in the first part of the Treaty of Rome.[4] Article 2 spells out that the establishment of a Common Market and the progressive approximation of the economic policies of the Member States are simply means to an end. The end is the promotion of a harmonious development of economic activities; a continuous and balanced expansion; an increase in stability; a raising of the standard of living and closer relations between the Member States.

The methods to be employed to bring this about are set out in Article 3. They include the free movement of goods, persons, services and capital, a common system of regulation of competition and common agricultural and transport policies. These are all being pursued. Thus internal quotas and industrial tariffs have been abolished. The right of freedom of establishment has been the subject of Directives, some of which have been implemented by the Member States. In addition to the specific provisions of the Treaty there are certain general provisions which aim at approximation of provisions which directly affect the setting up or operation of the Common Market (Article 100) or preventing discrepancies (Article 101) or distortions interfering with competition (Article 102). Moreover, Article 220 provides that Member States shall engage in negotiations for the reciprocal treatment of nationals, the elimination of double taxation, the mutual recognition of companies and the enforcement of foreign judgments. To this extent since January 1, 1973 the United Kingdom has by its membership of the Communities cut down its capacity for independent national law reform. It must now positively carry out the provisions of the Treaty of Rome and avoid innovations which are inconsistent therewith. Thus the area of national law reform has been reduced. Customs duties, agriculture, movement of labour and capital, transport, monopolies and restrictive practices and taxes are now excluded.[5] It is, however, easy to over-emphasise the extent of the actual area.[6] The large area of private law in which the Law Commission has mainly been operating to date is not directly affected for the time being. Much of it probably will never be affected even if closer political union comes about. However, the English Law Commission will, in common with other United Kingdom institutions, no doubt take more account of civil law concepts and principles even in this area in the future.

UNCITRAL, the Council of Europe and the European Communities are merely examples, for activities of this sort are the concern of many of the specialised agencies, of subsidiary organs of the United Nations and to some extent of the political alliances (*e.g.* NATO's Committee on Road Safety). Most of these bodies are dealing with problems of harmonising substantive laws. At the level of private international law or conflict of laws much progress is being made. One successful forum for such work is the Hague Conference on Private International Law. Its eleventh session in 1968, for instance, dealt with the problem of recognition of divorces and legal separations, adopting a draft convention on these topics.[7]

From the point of view of such a conference the problem of harmonisation or ultimately unification is one of comparing the various national models employed by Member States and selecting a model to be adopted by all participating states from one or more of these or, often, seeking some other appropriate and acceptable model. Such model is then set out in a convention or treaty to which participating states adhere. From the point of view of an individual participating state the problem may often be seen as one of "ordinary" domestic law reform although with powerful political reasons for adopting the model selected by the Conference. This can be illustrated by the way the United Kingdom Government dealt with the draft Convention approved by the Hague Conference mentioned above. The matter was referred to the Law Commissions to consider and report. They reported in favour of the international agreement with some additions[8] and proposed a draft Bill to alter the law accordingly. This has now been enacted as the Recognition of Divorces and Legal Separations Act 1971. Prior to the creation of the Law Commissions as we saw in Chapter 1 such things were entrusted to the Private International Law Committee.[9]

Essentially, therefore, the only matter in reform of sep-

arate legal orders which is additional to the considerations
which are relevant to ordinary municipal law reform is the
sometimes intractable problem of agreeing a common model.
The final choice in such matters is often based on political
or diplomatic rather than purely legal considerations. This
is the case for instance with the adoption by the United
Kingdom of Value Added Tax in place of Purchase Tax and
Selective Employment Tax in order to facilitate its entry
into the European Communities.

The question of the harmonisation of the rules of private
international law has recently been the subject of the Law
Commissions' Third Programme published in June 1973.
In this the commissioners referred to the invitation made
by the Benelux countries in 1967 to the Commission of the
EEC to undertake the unification of the private international law of the then Member States, which had as its aim
ultimate codification. The Commission thought that the
project as a whole was too ambitious but agreed that harmonisation in some areas would facilitate the working of
the Common Market and would bring greater benefits in
future as international legal (especially economic) relation-
ships increased. In January 1970 the six Member States
charged the working group on private international law in
Brussels with the task of preparing a series of Conventions
to harmonise the law on certain topics. In the summer of
1972 the group settled the text of a preliminary draft of the
Convention on the law applicable to obligations both con-
tractual and non-contractual. Further work has been started
on a draft Convention on the law applicable to corporeal
and incorporeal property.

In the light of this situation and upon our entry into the
EEC the Lord Chancellor asked the Law Commission to
consider the best method of examining the draft Conventions. A similar request was made by the Lord Advocate to
the Scottish Law Commission. The Law Commission real-
ized the need for reform preferably on an agreed interna-

tional basis. They noted the work done by the group and also by the Hague Conference on Private International Law. They therefore decided that in co-operation with the Scottish Law Commission they would appoint a joint working party to take such matters under review. This becomes Item No. XXI in the programme.

In addition, Mr. Norman Marsh Q.C. has served on the Kilbrandon Committee on the EEC Convention on the Enforcement and Recognition of Judgments. Members of the Law Commission are to be included from time to time in United Kingdom delegations attending international conferences on international harmonisation projects.

Reform of the international legal order on the other hand poses problems of a different and weightier kind. Here the law reformer has to deal with a distinct legal order of a primitive nature. The need for reform and codification of international law was foreseen by Jeremy Bentham in the eighteenth century.[10] It has become particularly acute recently with the creation of an increasing number of states in the aftermath of colonialism. The matter was one of the functions of the League of Nations and since then has become the more active concern of the United Nations Organisation. Article 19 of the League's convenant was rather restricted in scope. It merely stated that the Assembly "may from time to time advise the reconsideration ... of treaties which have become inapplicable." A resolution[11] passed in the Assembly on September 22, 1924 envisaged the creation of a standing committee to be called the Committee of Experts for the Progressive Codification of International Law to comprise representatives of "the main forms of civilization and the principal legal systems of the world." This committee was to prepare a list of subjects, the regulation of which by international agreement was desirable and realisable, to consider the comments of governments and their report. This was the first attempt on a worldwide basis to codify and develop whole areas of international law rather than simply regulating individual and specific legal problems. Under the League's auspices the Hague Conference of 1930 was convened but this was relatively unsuccessful, concluding agreements of only limited importance on one of the four issues before it.

The draftsmen of the Charter of the United Nations recognised the importance of international law reform[12] and mandated the new General Assembly in the following terms:

"The General Assembly shall initiate studies and make recommendations for the purpose of:
(a) ... encouraging the progressive development of international law and its codification."[13]

To this end the first session of the General Assembly set up a Committee on the Progressive Development of International Law and its Codification.[14] This Committee, of which J. L. Brierly was the rapporteur, reported the following June with the recommendation of the establishment of an International Law Commission (hereinafter called "the I.L.C."). Accordingly in November 1974, the General Assembly established the I.L.C. by resolution.[15] The body thereby established was a commission of fifteen part-time members, elected by the General Assembly from "persons of recognised competence in international law" for periods of office of three years. The growth in size of the United Nations has caused the number to be revised upwards in two stages to the present number of twenty-five. The other change, an increase in the length of tenure of office to five years, came as a result of the recognition of the difficult task before the commission. Like all other United Nations bodies, there has also been an amendment by resolution to the general wording of Article 2 (which deals with membership by regional distribution) by which Africa gets four seats, North America two, South America two, Asia six, Western Europe and others six, Eastern Europe three; including at every election the permanent members of the Security Council. It is thus broadly representative of potential conflicting interests.

The object of the I.L.C. was defined[16] as "the promotion of the progressive development of international law, and its codification," and it is provided that the commission "shall concern itself primarily with public international law, but is not precluded from entering the field of private international law." (While it could be argued that "private international law" is not international law within the sense of Article 13.1 of the United Nations Charter, which words are repeated as the object of the I.L.C., it is clearly within the competence of the United Nations General Assembly to set up a body to investigate private international law if it so desires. In practice the I.L.C. has never paid any attention to private international law.)

"Progressive development" (a pair of words deliberately chosen by the drafters as being more moderate than "revision," which overemphasised change) is defined as meaning "the preparation of draft conventions on subjects which have not yet been regulated by international law or in regard to which the law has not yet been sufficiently developed in the practice of states"[17] whereas codification meant "the more precise formulation and systematisation of rules of international law in fields where there already has been extensive state practice." This seems to separate the law-creating function of the I.L.C. from the law-declaring function, and restrict the former only to areas where no clear law exists. In practice, this was not intended to be the case, nor has it been the case. Indeed the I.L.C. has itself commented that this is a distinction that "can hardly be maintained."[18]

Nevertheless the statute lays down differing procedures which are to be followed for the two functions. When dealing with the progressive development of law the I.L.C. has to take its lead from its master. Upon a reference, the I.L.C. is required to consult with governments, then draft a report or convention. This is referred back to the governments for further consideration. The I.L.C. then reconsider the draft in the light of any comments and forward it with its recommendations to the General Assembly. Additionally, it may also consider any proposals for development by states or official inter-governmental bodies, and seek comments on them from governments, and then report to the General Assembly, seeking their "invitation" to continue the work if it so wishes.[19]

In the case of codification, the initiative rests more firmly with the I.L.C. It "shall survey the whole field of international law with a view to selecting topics for codification"[20] and recommend to the General Assembly accordingly. In pursuance of this the I.L.C., in the report on its first session, identified fourteen such areas (recognition, succession, Jurisdictional immunities, jurisdiction with regard to extra-territorial crime, high seas, territorial waters, nationality, treatment of aliens, asylum, treaties, diplomatic immunities, consular immunities, state responsibility, arbitral procedure). These have since been studied by the I.L.C. on their own initiative, in that the form of the report to the General Assembly is that of draft articles with a detailed commentary, *i.e.* after all the work has been done.

In so doing the I.L.C. may recommend that the General Assembly[21]:

(a) take no action, the report having been published;
(b) take note of or adopt the report;
(c) recommend the draft to members with a view to the conclusion of a convention;
(d) convoke a conference to conclude a convention.

The Commission also has a further power and function, "to consider ways and means for making evidence of customary international law more readily available." This power stems from special considerations, largely applicable only to international law, facing the reformer or codifier. The main sources of international law are treaties, customary law, and "general principles of law recognised by civilised states."[22] While of these, treaties provide clear rules, it is sometimes extremely difficult to deduce what customary rules, if any, have developed to cover a legal situation. To be classed as law, the rule in question must be the result of state practice such that the states consider themselves bound to follow the practice. The first issue is, therefore, to see what state practice is and what reasons motivate the practice. This necessary first step is often rendered difficult for the lawyer because of the lack of source material. For a variety of reasons most governments show extreme reluctance in articulating reasons for their foreign policy and, indeed, in putting on record further than necessary, what that policy is. Even where acts are "on the record," as for instance where one state recognises another, the reasons for and underlying criteria of such acts deliberately remain hidden.

To help combat this, the I.L.C. recommended the publication of its yearbook, the United Nations Juridical Yearbook, and the United Nations Legislative Series to assist in the spread of knowledge, and sought the General Assembly's assistance in the promotion of national volumes of practice in international law.

How successful is the I.L.C.?[23] Taken on the items it itself wished to work on, *i.e.* the codification measures, it has shown a high degree of success. Such codification would seem to be an essential pre-requisite to the development of international adjudication. It is only by making the rules of international law more certain and evident that states can be encouraged to undertake judicial settlement of disputes.[24] It is interesting to note, however, that the I.L.C. has failed to meet the demands specifically made of it in the earlier years by the General Assembly. References inspired by political or diplomatic reasons, rather than legal factors, are still political at the stage of reference back. For example, the General Assembly in 1949 asked the I.L.C. to consider (a) Draft Declaration on the Rights and Duties of States; (b)

Formulation of the Nürnburg Principles; (c) Draft Code of Offences Against the Peace and Security of Mankind; (d) Desirability and possibility of Establishing International Criminal Jurisdiction. (a) on reference back was commended by the General Assembly to members, who did nothing about it; (b) became tangled up in (c); (c) and (d) both were postponed from year to year until finally postponed *sine die* by the General Assembly in 1957 over the issue of defining aggression, a point still occupying a space in the United Nations' agenda.[25] On the other hand, consideration of nationality led to international conferences in 1959 and 1961, the latter adopting the Convention on the Reduction of Statelessness, based on a Commission draft. It should be noted here that the 1958 Convention on the Nationality of Married Women was adopted after negative advice by I.L.C. who decided that the issue should wait and take its part in a general treaty. Since then the pragmatic approach has had more appeal for the I.L.C. On the law of the sea, the I.L.C. was able to adopt articles on the Continental Shelf in 1953, and articles on the conservation of resources, the high seas, and the territorial sea by 1956. It recommended an international conference of plenipotentiaries to the General Assembly, who accepted and set up the 1958 Geneva Conference, leading to the adoption of the four Conventions of the Law of the Sea, which have received wide acceptance.

Arbitral procedure was also the subject of a report in the form of draft articles. This was referred by the General Assembly back to the I.L.C. who then took the line that they were preparing model rules for adoption by member states when appropriate. This set of model rules was recommended by the General Assembly to members "for their consideration and use, in such cases and to such extent as they consider appropriate."[26]

The I.L.C. also selected diplomatic immunities as an initial topic. The General Assembly in 1952 urged the acceleration of this item, which was started in 1954, and led to draft articles being sent to the General Assembly in 1958. This again led to a diplomatic conference, the Vienna Conference of 1961, which adopted the Vienna Convention on Diplomatic Relations, now ratified by over 100 states. The I.L.C., however, excepted from this item consideration of special missions and the relations between states and international bodies. A Convention on Special Missions, based on an I.L.C. draft was accepted by the General Assembly in 1969 without a conference, and articles on the relationship of representatives of states to international organisations were sent to the General Assembly in 1971. Work on consular relations led to an international conference in Vienna in 1963 and the Vienna Convention on Consular Relations.

The Law of Treaties had to wait until 1959 to take its place on the agenda of subjects being actively considered. The subject was "pruned" in that the I.L.C. left on one side the issues of (a) state responsibility for a breach of a treaty; (b) state succession to treaties; (c) the most favoured nation clause; (d) treaties involving international organisations. Draft articles again led to a Vienna Conference and the Vienna Convention on the Law of Treaties.

State responsibility, succession, the most favoured nation clause, treaties involving international organisations, are still on the agenda and two topics recently added by the General Assembly are the codification of the rules dealing with international waterways and the protection of diplomats.[27]

Is this a significant contribution? This can hardly be doubted. The solutions have not been perfect or final, as is shown by the convocation of another conference on the law of the sea scheduled to be held in 1974, and the reference of the issue of diplomatic protection to the I.L.C. in 1972 as an area not covered in previous consideration. It has however been responsible for the opening to signature of eight conventions on three major areas of practical importance. Such conventions acquire a momentum in international affairs and often have effects wider than signatures of the treaties necessarily show. For example, the United Kingdom ratified the Convention on Diplomatic Relations. In order to give effect to it the Diplomatic Privileges Act 1964 was passed, giving the status of English law to those articles of the treaty scheduled to the Act. But force of law was given to them as against all other countries, not just on a reciprocal basis.

Again there has been controversy over the extent to which such conventions can mould customary law to the same shape. It is clear that the International Court of Justice, after its judgment in the North Sea Continental Shelf cases,[28] is prepared to see this happen in appropriate cases.

By concentrating with, one must feel, more than an eye to the political and diplomatic significance of the items selected, on issues such as the law of treaties, the I.L.C. has built up a reputation both for itself and, of infinitely more significance, for international law as a means of regulating international conduct. It has circumvented such intractable problems as the width of the territorial seas and, so far, the question of the breach of treaties, and has clarified the law relating to other issues. This has thrown the areas of disagreement into sharp contrast with the generality of the accepted rules in each field and, whilst not thereby solving the controversies, has procured consideration of them at a rational level.

Notes

[1] United Nations General Assembly Resolution 2205 (XXI) (1966).

[2] See generally A. H. Robertson, *The Council of Europe* and *European Institutions* (3rd ed.), Chap. 2.

[3] See Robertson *European Institutions*, p. 60. See further the bulletins issued by the Council—"Forward in Europe" and "Legal Co-operation in Europe."

[4] See Professor D. Lasok and J. W. Bridge's *Introduction to the Law and Institutions of the European Communities*, Chap. 2 and Professor P. S. R. F. Mathijsen's *Guide to European Community Law*,

p. 6 for discussions of the juridical status of the Community.

[5] See "Legal and Constitutional Implications of United Kingdom Membership of the European Communities" Cmnd. 3301 (1967), paras. 25 *et seq.*

[6] Although at least one distinguished continental jurist has said that in matters coming within the ambit of the Treaty, independent national law reform might be against the spirit if not the letter of the Treaty: see Bärman, "Iste eine Aktienrechtsreform überhaupt noch zulässig" [1959] *Juristenzeitung* 434.

[7] See Morris, *The Conflict of Laws*, p. 149.

[8] Law Com. No. 34; Scot. Law Com. No. 16.

[9] See, *e.g.* their fourth report Cmnd. 491 (1958) which led to the Wills Act 1963.

[10] See his *Principles of International Law* (1786).

[11] League of Nations' Official Journal, Special Supplement, No. 21, p. 10.

[12] See *The Work of the International Law Commission* published by the U.N. Office of Public Information, p. 3.

[13] See *op. cit.*, p. 4, and Herbert W. Briggs, *The International Law Commission*, Part I for detailed discussion.

[14] General Assembly Resolution 94 (I) (1946).

[15] General Assembly Resolution 174 (II) (1947). The statute of the I.L.C. is an annex to the resolution.

[16] Art. 1.

[17] Art. 15.

[18] Report of 8th Session II, 255, 26.

[19] Arts. 16 and 17.

[20] Art. 18.

[21] Art. 25.

[22] Art. 38(1). Statute of the International Court of Justice.

[23] See Professor Julius Stone's sad commentary on the I.L.C. in "On the Vocation of the International Law Commission" (1957) 57 Col. L.R. 16, 48-49. *Cf.* however, Luke T. Lee, "The International Law Commission Re-examined" (1965) 59 A.J.I.L. 545.

[24] See Lee, *op. cit.*, p. 546. See also Herbert W. Briggs' comments in "Reflections on the Codification of International Law by the International Law Commission and by other agencies" 126 *Hague Recueil* 233-316.

[25] See also the activities of the highly political Special Committee on the Principles of International Law Concerning Friendly Relations and Co-operation among States in Briggs, "Reflections," *op. cit.*, p. 284.

[26] 1262 (XIII) (1958).

[27] For a discussion of the work of the 1972 session of the I.L.C. see Kearney in (1973) 67 A.J.I.L. 84.

[28] [1969] I.C.J. Rep. 16.

CHAPTER 9

THE END OF THE BEGINNING

At the time of writing the English Law Commission has published its Seventh Annual Report,[1] and there has been the change in personnel mentioned in Chapter 5. It seems a reasonable time to take stock of the Commission's achievements so far and to speculate on the future.

The Commission's productivity has been impressive. The legislation resulting from its reports is shown in Appendix E. Its productivity is all the more remarkable considering its size. As Professor Geoffrey Sawer in a stimulating and thought provoking article[2] has pointed out, it is "a modest concern whether regarded as a government instrumentality or as a legal partnership; it is comparable with the provincial branch of a revenue department or one medium Wall Street firm or one largish London or Melbourne or Toronto Solicitor's office." On the face of it, it looks like law reform on the cheap but on the other hand size tends to breed bureaucracy which in its turn breeds conservatism. The paucity of reform emanating from the Department of Trade and Industry on company law and bankruptcy until recently is perhaps an example of this.[3]

The high productivity of the first six years, however, appears to have slowed down and there are signs of some institutional introspection. It is likely that this has partly arisen from the change of personnel and their re-examination of the programmes devised by the earlier team. In the Annual Report of *Justice* for 1973 Lord Gardiner

who obviously has a vested interest in the success of the Law
Commissions wrote that "In general the climate for reform,
except where commendable to the Government, is not as
favourable as it might be." It is obvious that the Government
do not share Lord Gardiner's own great enthusiasm for
reform and the present Lord Chancellor may be reflecting, as
he is apt to do, on the example of his father[4] who had shown
similar scepticism at the enthusiasm of Lord Sankey in the
1930s.

One matter upon which the Law Commission has been
criticised by Professor Gordon Borrie[5] is the question of
priorities in its programmes. Professor Borrie felt that time
had been spent on patchwork reforms and tidying up the
Statute Book instead of going back to first principles and
re-examining the basic concepts and principles of the law.
In the writer's view this criticism is unjust. The Law Commission is right to tackle things in the way it has. A more
fundamental reappraisal of the ambitious kind envisaged
by Professor Borrie can come later. In any event such a task
as he envisaged would be better initiated in the universities
in the first instance and it is perhaps a criticism of them that
it has not been done. A more telling criticism, however, made
by Professor Borrie is that the Law Commission has concen-
trated too much on the reform of substantive law at the expense of procedure. The points which he makes about the
limits of the Legal Aid scheme and Small Claims Courts have
been mitigated to a certain extent by recent reforms but
the basic dissatisfaction with civil litigation to which he refers
needs attention. The Report of the *Justice* Committee under
the chairmanship of Lord Devlin may produce some of the
ideas which have so far been lacking from the Law Commission.

Should all the Law Commissioners be full time? In the
case of practitioners they may lose touch or find it difficult
to return to practice. Perhaps practitioner-commissioners
should be part time. However, five years is not a very long

time and on the whole part-timers are perhaps best employed on specialist committees or as consultants. According to its latest report the Law Commission is making increasing use of part-timers in this way. It is probably largely for this reason that the Law Reform Committee and the Criminal Law Revision Committee have been retained. Nevertheless the use of part-timers can have drawbacks particularly on a long term project such as codification which necessarily involves many meetings and familiarity with the cluster of interlocking concepts and rules which the preparation of a code necessarily engenders.

At the time of its creation there was some criticism that the Act did not allow for lay Law Commissioners.[6] There is some force in this criticism[7] and parliamentary debate is not necessarily a substitute. However, Sir Leslie Scarman in an article in the *American Bar Journal* in 1971[8] answered the criticisms in this way. The day to day work of a law reform agency is largely a research and drafting routine. In this routine sociologists or other laymen "would have to play a waiting game. Their contribution to law reform appears to us to come at the stage when initial research has provided a description of the law as it is and a provisional identification of the matters requiring reform. At this stage laymen and members of other disciplines have a vital part to play; they may well see injustices or anomalies not evident to the unaided eye of the lawyer." Further as Geoffrey Sawer points out "it is difficult to believe that a lay commissioner could either represent the infinite diversity of lay interests in law reform or usefully participate in the cut and thrust of Commission debate on legal technicalities." Lay men are probably best coopted on to specialist committees on the basis of their expertise rather than as "statutory lay men."

Turning from personnel to methods, the present system of working papers seems on the whole to work well. Nevertheless consultation tends largely to be with pressure groups. In many cases this is inevitable but it is not necessarily so.

In their latest report the Law Commission say they intend to use more social surveys presumably to explore social facts and popular values. Consultation might be extended on certain topics to follow the example of royal commissions, certain of the Canadian law commissions and American legislative committees in having public hearings. Law Commission staff could conduct these hearings. The Manitoba Law Commission advertises its proposals and solicits views by advertisements in layman's language in the popular press.

Although the Law Commission has been successful to date in achieving parliamentary enactment of its proposals this may not always be the case. There is no fixed procedure. Sir Leslie Scarman on a number of occasions has suggested that perhaps we need a Ministry of Justice after all and as we have seen such a Ministry works well in a common law jurisdiction such as New Zealand.[9] The main trouble, however, with the long debate on the utility of a Ministry of Justice in the United Kingdom is that conceptions of such a Ministry have changed during the debate. In many ways, given the untidyness of the present system, with an expanded Lord Chancellor's department, active involvement in reform by some of the ministries and the Law Commission and two other permanent law reform bodies we have most of what Bentham, Austin, Langdale and Westbury called for in such a Ministry. Also the British system of government has developed in such a way that the establishment of a body with some of the powers of the French *Conseil d'Etat* would be a retrograde step. The *Curia Regis* as such is lost in the mists of English legal history.[10] As we have seen, the "Law Reform —Now" proposals[11] favoured a Vice-Chancellor in the House of Commons and despite Lord Fletcher's scepticism on the utility of such an office in the long term[12] it is suggested that a third law officer on these lines is what is needed rather than a Ministry of Justice on the New Zealand pattern and that a Vice-Chancellor, rather than the Lord Chancellor, should be the Minister with overall responsibility for law reform.[13] Law reform is inadequately represented in the House of Commons. Also, following the New Zealand precedent, the Vice-Chancellor should *ex officio* be a member of the Law Commission but, unlike that system, in some purely nominal and titular capacity such as President or Convenor. It would seem that by the latter the measure of independence already enjoyed by the Law Commission would not be sacrificed and an established entrée into Parliament would be gained.[14] This would, however, necessitate amendments to the Law Commissions Act 1965.

Considering its size the Law Commission seems to have been a little naïve in favouring widespread codification. As we have seen opinions differ on what form a code should take but everyone concedes that it is a time consuming project. It has been suggested by one learned commentator that the Law Commission's recommendations should be aimed at the judges rather than the legislature for the judges to fashion into the case law.[15] It is submitted that a compromise might be on the lines of a suggestion considered by the committee which made proposals for setting up the American Law Institute[16]—namely that the principles put forward should not be enacted as an ordinary statute but should be enacted to have the status of a series of *rationes decidendi* of the House of Lords which could be extended by the courts and form the basis of statutory analogies which so far the common law, unlike the civil law, has found inimical. It should, however, be clearly provided that the House of Lords should, notwithstanding the 1966 Direction,[17] not have authority to overrule such statutory provisions. The question arises whether these should follow the normal parliamentary procedures. Lord Devlin[18] has suggested a limited law-making power for the Law Commissions by means of delegated legislation. On the whole, however, it would seem preferable to have some modified form of parliamentary procedure for the scrutiny and adoption of such legislation.[19]

The whole subject of the form and language of legislation

generally needs thorough investigation by the Renton Committee. Compared with much Common Market legislation many of our statutes appear labyrinthine. It is submitted that one approach might be to consider first of all whether different forms and styles of legislation are needed for different areas of law.[20]

The creation and operation of the Law Commissions have necessarily had some impact on the judiciary. Sometimes this has been exaggerated. At the risk of appearing simplistic let us briefly consider the nature of the judges' role. Their primary role is to decide cases. It is now orthodox theory that this is not a mechanistic function and that judges, applying statute and case law to fact situations, do perform a role which is often creative. Large areas of English law have in the past been judge-made. In recent years the judiciary have served on official law reform bodies which have led to law reform legislation.

Since the Law Commissions were created the judiciary have continued to decide cases and have continued their law-making function. They have also continued as individuals to fall between the two poles of judicial liberalism and conservatism. Some have been open about their law-making function; some have played it down using the traditional clichés. There has, however, been an increasing feeling in recent years by some leading judges that their law-making activities should now be curtailed to some extent. The only question is, to what extent? Thus in a broadcast discussion in 1969 Lord Devlin[21] said "My idea of a healthy judiciary is a judiciary that is not concerned with where the law leads it ... Until your statute law is well drawn and comprehensively drawn, I myself fear judicial intervention in the process of law reform." This echoes views which he expressed before the creation of the Law Commissions in the Preface to *Samples of Law Making*—"The judges always have been and still are fashioners of law, not creators, out of the material that is supplied to them ... In the early days of the common law the judges had to do much of their own spinning; today the legislative mills turn out the yarn in great quantities and in varying qualities but it still has to be woven into cloth."[22] Again in an address entitled "Law in a Restless Society" given to the Annual General Meeting of *Justice* in 1972 he said it was the function of the judiciary to administer the law not to make it although it was always difficult to avoid some element of law-making. The trouble was that the judiciary had never really disentangled itself from its old role when judges were servants of the Crown. Their role had political implications which had survived in the office of Lord Chancellor. Even Lord Denning[23] has recognised that the scope of judicial law-making is now cut down although he argues that even with the Law Commission there is still a need for it.

Mr. Norman Marsh Q.C.[24] has identified five factors about judicial law reform which make it unsatisfactory. First, the reforming decision is quite fortuitous in its operation. The public may have to wait many years before an appropriate opportunity arises in the courts. In the words of Lord Devlin the law has to "await a litigant with a long purse or the Legal Aid Fund behind him."[25] Secondly, judge-made reforms, until finally approved at the highest level, are of uncertain stability. He instances the classic example of deserted wife's equity. Thirdly, the court carries out a patching job and generally cannot consider the impact on the law as a whole. Law reform agencies have more time and the advantages of consultation. Fourthly, law reform in the courts might be unjust for one of the parties who finds the law changes retrospectively and fifthly, and perhaps most importantly, it is no longer possible for the judge in modern English society "to make those bold assumptions about family life and about relations between landlord and tenant, employer and employee, citizen and state which underlie many reforms of a seemingly legal character. On the one hand he lives in an era where many value assumptions are being challenged; on the other, he does not enjoy quite the unquestioned prestige, the charismatic authority, enjoyed by his Victorian forbears."[26]

One major part of the Law Commissions' activities which as we have seen could affect the judiciary in the long term is codification. Sir Leslie Scarman thought that this would mean that the contribution of the judges to the law would change. "They will lose their priestly character as oracles drawing from within upon the experience of themselves and their predecessors in office to declare the law; they will stand forth as the authoritative interpreters of the code."[27] Some commentators point to the role of the judiciary in France as evidence that the English judiciary will suffer a *capitis diminutio*. The analogy of French law needs to be treated with caution. First, the schizophrenic attitude reflected in articles 4 and 5 of the French Civil Code was the product of political hostility to the judiciary of the *ancien regime*.[28] Secondly the judiciary in France are different from English judges in their historical background, training and social status. There is not the same concept of what an American writer described of the "judge as hero,"[29] which still exists to some extent in the common law world. Thirdly, despite the theory, the practice shows that French judges do make law under the guise of interpretation.[30]

It is suggested, however, that further consideration needs to be given to the role of the judiciary in law reform and their relationship with the Law Commission. Once again we turn to the ideas of Sir Leslie Scarman. In his article "Inside the English Law Commission" in the American Bar Association Journal in 1971[31] he wrote "The fact is that the courts—although not openly announcing it as their policy—have recognized that there are certain areas of the law in which they must continue to make creative decisions. These are areas of the law which the Law Commission does not have under review or is unlikely to have under review for some time." It is suggested that this is not so much a description of what the judges are doing as the basis of a prescription of what they ought to do. Also where necessary legislation is delayed the courts might make greater use of the Law Commission's reports as doctrine or *ratio legis*. Let us use by analogy the idea of Karl Popper,[32] that the activity of understanding is a species of problem-solving, producing hypotheses which are valid until falsified. The courts are faced with problems to solve. The Law Commissions are producing hypotheses to solve the problems which the courts can test as appropriate in the circumstances of a particular case. The analogy ignores the normative character of law but is only proffered as an analogy to illumine the nature of the new partnership which should evolve between the courts and the Law Commissions.

In a lecture given to the Bentham Club in 1951 entitled "The Need for a New Equity"[33] Sir Alfred Denning (as he then was) asked where the new equity was to be found. The answer then, he thought, lay in "the new spirit which is alive in our universities." It would appear, however, that the "spirit" has now been institutionalised in a more practical way by the Law Commission which, although performing a different role in the legal system from the Court of Chancery, is the source of new ideas of fairness in administration of the law. Nevertheless in the evolution of those ideas academic lawyers have an increasingly important role to play.

In conclusion, however, it might be said with regret that the Law Commission has probably been created too late in the day. The ambitious programme of rationalisation should have preceded rather than followed our entry into the Common Market. The opportunities to reform and simplify the substantive law in the late nineteenth and early twentieth centuries were wasted. Now the accelerated programme of simplification and reform and the combination of changes in the law necessitated by both the Law Commission and the Common Market create an exceptionally heavy burden on the practitioner and the public. Further, since January 1, 1973 by adopting the Treaty of Rome and joining the European Economic Community we have fettered our right of independent national law reform at least in respect of some of the matters covered by the Treaty and to that extent the powers of the Law Commission are curtailed.[34] Sooner or later we may have a European Law Commission.[35] English law reform has now acquired a European and indeed an international dimension.

Notes

[1] Law Com. No. 50. See the leader in *The Times* of December 15, 1972, and the interview of Scarman L.J.—"The Future of the English Judge" in *The Sunday Times* of December 17, 1972. See further Appendix F.

[2] "The Legal Theory of Law Reform" (1970) 20 University of Toronto L.J. 183.

[3] See Lord Gardiner, "The Role of the Lord Chancellor in the field of Law Reform" (1971) 87 L.Q.R. 326, 335

[4] See *The Listener* July 13, 1972, p. 42.

[5] "Law Reform: A Damp Squib"—inaugural lecture at the University of Birmingham 1970.

[6] See Chapter 4.

[7] See Sawer, *op. cit.*, p. 194.

[8] "Inside the English Law Commission" (1971) 57 A.B.A.J. 867.

[9] See *Law Reform—the New Pattern*. See also the transcript of the JUSTICE conference "Do we need a Ministry of Justice?" especially Sir George Coldstream at pp. 12-18; Geoffrey Howe at pp. 34-39; Peter Archer at pp. 40-45; Andrew Martin at pp. 52-55; and Sir Leslie Scarman's summing up at pp. 60 *et seq.* However for some second thoughts see Sir Leslie's article in (1971) 57 A.B.J. 867, 869.

[10] *Ibid.*, p. 8.

[11] *Cf.* Andrew Martin Q.C. in *Methods of Law Reform* (1967).

[12] See Chapter 3 but see also Alan Watkins in the *New Statesman*, July 13, 1973, p. 38 for an attack on the Law Officers and a case for a Ministry of Justice.

[13] See the report of the Society of Conservative Lawyers on "Ministerial Responsibility for Law" (1971).

[14] See the views of Sir Leslie Scarman in "The English Law Commission" (1972) 1 *Anglo-American Law Review* 31, 40.

[15] See R. J. Sutton, "The English Law Commission: a New Philosophy of Law Reform" (1967) 20 Vanderbilt L.R. 1009, 1020.

[16] See their report discussed in Chapter 7.

[17] [1966] 3 All E.R. 77; [1966] 1 W.L.R. 1234.

[18] "The Process of Law Reform" (1966) 63 L.S.Gaz. 333.

[19] See Scarman, *Codification and Judge-Made Law*, p. 21.

[20] See generally Chapter 5.

[21] See *What's Wrong with the Law?* (ed. Michael Zander), pp. 91 and 93.

[22] *Ibid.*, p. 3. See also Wedderburn, "Reflections on Law Reform," *The Listener*, May 6, 1965, p. 685—"now that the policy implications of their decisions are receiving open study [the judges'] development of the law must not reflect a separate social policy and must take heed both of Parliament and of its Law Commission."

[23] *Sunday Times*, June 24, 1973. See also *R.* v. *Bow Road Domestic Court* [1968] 2 All E.R. 89, 93 and *Breen* v. *Amalgamated Engineering Workers* [1971] 2 W.L.R. 742, 753

[24] *What's wrong with the Law?*, pp. 29-32 and his paper "Law Reform in the United Kingdom, A New Institutional Approach" in (1971) 13 William and Mary L.R. 263, 266 *et seq.* For a discussion of the drawbacks of judicial law-making in connection with the deserted wife's equity see the remarks of Megarry J. in *Wroth* v. *Tyler* [1973] 1 All E.R. 897, 906 where he says "one difficulty of the courts dealing with the matter was that any doctrine evolved by the courts was likely to take many years and much litigation involving heavy costs, before a workable doctrine emerged in an established and fully fledged form; and there was much uncertainty about many features of the equity ... Statute could avoid all the difficulties, expense and delays of a doctrine evolved by the courts by laying down a complete system *uno ictu*. In truth, the institution of what might amount to a new right of priority, however badly needed, is a reform which the courts are ill-equipped to make."

[25] (1971) 13 William and Mary L.R. 266.

[26] *Op. cit.*, p. 4.

[27] *Codification and Judge-Made Law*, p. 11

[28] See Von Mehren, *The Civil Law System*, pp. 839 *et seq.*; J. Vanderlinden, "Some Reflections on the Law-Making Powers of the French Judiciary" (1968) Juridical Review 1.

[29] See Franklin, "The Historic Function of the American Law Institute" (1934) 47 H.L.R. 1367, 1370.

[30] See, *e.g.* Mazeaud, *Leçons du Droit Civil*, Vol. 1, p. 116 and Juillot de la Morandière, *Droit Civil* (3rd ed.), Vol I, p. 86, and see generally Julius Stone, *Legal System and Lawyers' Reasonings*, pp. 212 *et seq.*—"Logic and Growth under a Code."

[31] (1971) 57 A.B.A.J. 867, 870. See the recent case of *Launchbury* v. *Morgan* [1973] A.C. 127 where the House of Lords have drawn the line in a similar way on an important question of social policy in relation to vicarious liability for car accidents. The speech of Lord Wilberforce is an important statement of the judges' role in relation to questions of social policy. See also Megarry J. in *Wroth* v. *Tyler* [1973] 1 All E.R. 897, 906 referred to above in fn. 24.

[32] See *Objective Knowledge*, Chapter 4—"On the Theory of the Objective Mind."

[33] (1952) 5 C.L.P. at p. 10

[34] See Chapter 8, *infra*. A distinguished continental jurist has

argued that any independent national law reform on matters falling within the scope of the Treaty of Rome is contrary to the spirit if not the letter of the Treaty. See Bärmann, "Iste eine Aktienrechtsreform überhaupt noch zulässig" [1959] *Juristenzeitung* 434. It should be noted, however, that this has not necessarily been heeded by some of the Member States—see *e.g.* the French company Law reforms of 1966 mentioned in H. J. Ault, "Harmonization of Company Law in the E.E.C." (1968) 20 Hastings L.J. 77.

[35] A proposal for such a Commission was made in a paper by S. C. Silken M.P. as Chairman of the Legal Committee of the Consultative Assembly to the Fifth Conference of European Ministers of Justice. See Professor J. D. B. Mitchell's "Why European Institutions?" in *European Law Institutions* by L. J. Brinkhorst and J. D. B. Mitchell, pp. 38 and 55.

DETAILS OF THE PERMANENT OFFICIAL LAW REFORM BODIES AS AT THE END OF 1972

A. Law Revision Committee appointed by Lord Sankey, January 10, 1934

Terms of reference: "To consider how far, having regard to the statute law and to judicial decisions, such legal maxims and doctrines as the Lord Chancellor may from time to time refer to the Committee require revision in modern conditions."

Details of Reports and their Implementation

First Report	1934 (Cmd. 4540)	*Actio personalis moritur cum persona.*	Law Reform (Miscellaneous Provisions) Act 1934.
Second Report	1934 (Cmd. 4546)	Right to recover interest in civil proceedings.	Law Reform (Miscellaneous Provisions) Act 1934.
Third Report	1934 (Cmd. 4637)	Doctrine of no contribution between tortfeasors.	Law Reform (Married Women and Joint Tortfeasors) Act 1935.

Fourth Report	1934 (Cmd. 4770)	Liability of the husband for the torts of the wife and liability of a married woman in tort and contract.	Law Reform (Married Women and Joint Tort-feasors) Act 1935.
Fifth Report	1936 (Cmd. 5334)	Statute of Limitations.	Limitation Act 1939.
Sixth Report	1937 (Cmd. 5449)	Statute of Frauds and the doctrine of consideration.	No action on either, but see B.
Seventh Report	1939 (Cmd. 6009)	The rule in *Chandler v. Webster* (frustration).	Law Reform (Frustrated Contracts) Act 1943.
Eighth Report	1939 (Cmd. 6032)	Contributory negligence.	Law Reform (Contributory Negligence) Act 1945.

B. Law Reform Committee appointed by Lord Simonds, June 16, 1952

Terms of reference: "To consider, having regard especially to judicial decisions, what changes are desirable in such legal doctrines as the Lord Chancellor may from time to time refer to the Committee."

Details of Reports and their Implementation

First Report	1953 (Cmd. 8809)	Statute of Frauds and section 4 of the Sale of Goods Act 1893.	Law Reform (Enforcement of Contracts) Act 1954.
Second Report	1954 (Cmd. 9161)	Innkeepers' liability for property of travellers, guests and residents.	Hotel Proprietors Act 1956.
Third Report	1954 (Cmd. 9305)	Occupiers' liability to invitees, licensees and trespassers.	Occupiers' Liability Act 1957.
Fourth Report	1956 (Cmd. 18)	The rule against perpetuities.	Perpetuities and Accumulations Act 1964.
Fifth Report	1957 (Cmd. 62)	Conditions and exceptions in insurance policies.	No action but none recommended.

Sixth Report	1957 (Cmd. 310)	Court's power to sanction variation of trusts.	Variation of Trusts Act 1958.
Seventh Report	1958 (Cmd. 501)	Effect of tax liability on damages.	No action recommended by majority.
Eighth Report	1958 (Cmd. 622)	Sealing of contracts made by bodies corporate.	Corporate Bodies' Contracts Act 1960.
Ninth Report	1961 (Cmd. 1268)	Liability in tort between husband and wife.	Law Reform (Husband and Wife) Act 1962.
Tenth Report	1962 (Cmd. 1782)	Innocent misrepresentation.	Misrepresentation Act 1967.
Eleventh Report	1963 (Cmd. 2017)	Loss of services, etc.	No action.
Twelfth Report	1966 (Cmd. 2958)	Transfer of title to chattels.	No action.
Thirteenth Report	1966 (Cmd. 2964)	Hearsay evidence in civil proceedings.	Civil Evidence Act 1968.
Fourteenth Report	1966 (Cmd. 3100)	Acquisition of easements and profits by prescription.	No action.
Fifteenth Report	1967 (Cmd. 3391)	The rule in *Hollington v. Hewthorn*.	Civil Evidence Act 1968.
Sixteenth Report	1967 (Cmd. 3472)	Privilege in civil proceedings.	Civil Evidence Act 1968.

Seventeenth Report 1970 (Cmd. 4489)	Evidence of opinion and expert evidence.	Civil Evidence Act 1972.
Eighteenth Report 1971 (Cmd. 4774)	Conversion and detinue.	No action.
Nineteenth Report 1973 (Cmd. 5301)	Interpretation of wills.	No action.

C. Criminal Law Revision Committee appointed by R. A. Butler on February 2, 1959

Terms of reference: "To be a standing committee to examine such aspects of the criminal law of England and Wales as the Home Secretary may from time to time refer to the Committee, to consider whether the law requires revision and to make recommendations."

Details of Reports and their Implementation

First Report	Cmnd. 835 (1959)	Indecency with children.	The Indecency with Children Act 1960.
Second Report	Cmnd. 1187 (1960)	Suicide.	The Suicide Act 1961.
Third Report	Cmnd. 2149 (1963)	Criminal procedure (insanity).	The Criminal Procedure (Insanity) Act 1964.

Fourth Report	Cmnd. 2148 (1963)	Order of closing speeches.	The Criminal Procedure (Right of Reply) Act 1964.
Fifth Report	Cmnd. 2349 (1964)	Criminal procedure (jurors).	The Criminal Justice Act 1965.
Sixth Report	Cmnd. 2465 (1964)	Perjury and attendance of witnesses.	The Criminal Procedure (Attendance of Witnesses) Act 1965.
Seventh Report	Cmnd. 2659 (1965)	Felonies and misdemeanours.	The Criminal Law Act 1967.
Eighth Report	Cmnd. 2977 (1966)	Theft and related offences.	The Theft Act 1968.
Ninth Report	Cmnd. 3145 (1966)	Evidence (written statements, formal admissions and notices of alibi).	The Criminal Justice Act 1967.
Tenth Report	Cmnd. 3750 (1968)	Secrecy of jury room.	
Eleventh Report	Cmnd. 4991 (1972)	Evidence (general).	
Twelfth Report	Cmnd. 5184 (1973)	Penalty for murder.	

D. Private International Law Committee, 1952 (Lord Chancellor)—now moribund

Details of published reports

Law of Domicile, Cmmd. 9068 (1954).
Formal Validity of Wills, Cmmd. 491 (1958).
Foreign Arbitrary Awards, Cmmd. 1515 (1961).
Monetary Law, Cmmd. 1648 (1962).
Domicile, Cmmd. 1955 (1963).

E. The Law Commission created by the Law Commissions Act 1965

Terms of reference: see section 3 of the Act which is discussed in Chapter 4 (*infra*).

IMPLEMENTATION OF THE LAW COMMISSION'S PROPOSALS
AS AT THE DATE OF THE EIGHTH ANNUAL REPORT

Titles of relevant Reports	*Date of Publication*	*Implemented*
Proposals to abolish certain ancient criminal offences (Law Com. No. 3).	June 22, 1966	Criminal Law Act 1967 (c. 58).
Proposals for reform of the law relating to maintenance and champerty (Law Com. No. 7).	November 22, 1966	Criminal Law Act 1967 (c. 58).

Titles of relevant Reports	Date of Publication	Implemented
The powers of appeal courts to sit in private and the restrictions upon publicity in domestic proceedings (Law Com. No. 8).	November 23, 1966	Domestic and Appellate Proceedings (Restriction of Publicity) Act 1968 (c. 63).
Transfer of Land: interim report on root of title to freehold land (Law Com. No. 9).	February 14, 1967	Law of Property Act 1969 (c. 59).
Imputed criminal intent (*Director of Public Prosecutions* v. *Smith*) (Law Com. No. 10).	February 28, 1967	In part by section 8 of the Criminal Justice Act 1967 (c. 80).
Transfer of Land: report on restrictive covenants (Law Com. No. 11).	March 22, 1967	In part by Law of Property Act 1969 (c. 59).
Sea Fisheries (Shellfish) Bill (Joint report with Scottish Law Commission) (Law Com. No. 11A).	May 11, 1967	Sea Fish (Conservation) Act 1969 (c. 84).
Civil liability for animals (Law Com. No. 13).	December 21, 1967	Animals Act 1971 (c. 22).
Blood tests and the proof of paternity in civil proceedings (Law Com. No. 16).	October 31, 1968	Family Law Reform Act 1969 (c. 46).

Titles of relevant Reports	Date of Publication	Implemented
Landlord and Tenant: report on the Landlord and Tenant Act 1954, Part II (Law. Com. No. 17).	January 22, 1969	Law of Property Act 1969 (c. 59).
Transfer of Land: report on land charges affecting unregistered land (Law Com. No. 18).	March 20, 1969	Law of Property Act 1969 (c. 59).
Trustee Savings Banks Bill (Joint report with Scottish Law Commission) (Law Com. No. 18A).	April 17, 1969	Trustee Savings Banks Act 1969 (c. 50).
Proceedings against estates (Law Com. No. 19).	May 2, 1969	Proceedings Against Estates Act 1970 (c. 17).
Interpretation of statutes (Joint report with Scottish Law Commission) (Law. Com. No. 21).	June 11, 1969	No.
Statute Law Revision: first report (Law Com. No. 22).	July 8, 1969	Statute Law (Repeals) Act 1969 (c. 52).
Proposal for the abolition of the matrimonial remedy of restitution of conjugal rights (Law Com. No. 23).	August 26, 1969	Matrimonial Proceedings and Property Act 1970 (c. 45).

Titles of relevant Reports	Date of Publication	Implemented
Exemption clauses in contracts: first report. Amendments to the Sale of Goods Act 1893 (Joint report with Scottish Law Commission) (Law Com. No. 24).	September 18, 1969	Supply of Goods (Implied Terms) Act 1973 (c. 13).
Financial provision in matrimonial proceedings (Law Com. No. 25).	September 23, 1969	Matrimonial Proceedings and Property Act 1970 (c. 45); Law Reform (Miscellaneous Provisions) Act 1970 (c. 33).
Breach of promise of marriage (Law Com. No. 26).	October 15, 1969	Law Reform (Miscellaneous Provisions) Act 1970 (c. 33).
Statute Law Revision: second report. Draft Wild Creatures and Forest Laws Bill (Law Com. No. 28).	August 4, 1970	Wild Creatures and Forest Laws Act 1971 (c. 47).
Criminal Law: offences of damage to property (Law Com. No. 29).	September 16, 1970	Criminal Damage Act 1971 (c. 48).
Powers of attorney (Law Com. No. 30).	September 23, 1970	Powers of Attorney Act 1971 (c. 27).

Titles of relevant Reports	Date of Publication	Implemented
Administration bonds, personal representatives' rights of retainer and preference and related matters (Law Com. No. 31).	October 15, 1970	Administration of Estates Act 1971 (c. 25).
Nullity of marriage (Law Com. No. 33).	December 4, 1970	Nullity of Marriage Act 1971 (c. 44).
Hague Convention on Recognition of Divorces and Legal Separations (Joint report with Scottish Law Commission) (Law Com. No. 34).	December 1, 1970	Recognition of Divorces and Legal Separations Act 1971 (c. 53).
Limitation Act 1963 (Law Com. No. 35).	November 25, 1970	Law Reform (Miscellaneous Provisions Act 1971 (c. 43).
Statute Law Revision: third report. Draft Statute Law (Repeals) Bill (Law Com. No. 37).	December 15, 1970	Statute Law (Repeals) Act 1971 (c. 52).
Coinage Bill (Joint report with Scottish Law Commission) (Law Com. No. 38).	November 26, 1970	Coinage Act 1971 (c. 24).

Titles of relevant Reports	Date of Publication	Implemented
Vehicles (Excise) Bill (Joint report with Scottish Law Commission) (Law Com. No. 39).	December 2, 1970	Vehicles (Excise) Act 1971 (c. 10).
Civil liability of vendors and lessors for defective premises (Law Com. No. 40).	December 16, 1970	Defective Premises Act 1972 (c. 35).
National Savings Bank Bill (Joint report with Scottish Law Commission) (Law Com. No. 41).	January 13, 1971	National Savings Bank Act 1971 (c. 29).
Polygamous marriages (Law Com. No. 42).	February 3, 1971	Matrimonial Proceedings (Polygamous Marriages) Act 1972 (c. 38).
Taxation of income and gains derived from land (Joint report with Scottish Law Commission) (Law Com. No. 43).	April 28, 1971	In part by section 82 of the Finance Act 1972 (c. 41).
Town and Country Planning Bill (Law Com. No. 45).	June 10, 1971	Town and Country Planning Act 1971 (c. 78).
Road Traffic Bill (Joint report with Scottish Law Commission) (Law Com. No. 46).	July 26, 1971	Road Traffic Act 1972 (c. 20).

Titles of relevant Reports	Date of Publication	Implemented
Jurisdiction in matrimonial causes (Law Com. No. 48).	September 14, 1972	Domicile and Matrimonial Proceedings Act 1973 (c. 45).
Statute Law Revision: fourth report. Draft Statute Law (Repeals) Bill (Joint report with Scottish Law Commission) (Law Com. No. 49).	September 28, 1972	Statute Law (Repeals) Act 1973 (c. 39).
Matrimonial Causes Bill (Law Com. No. 51).	December 18, 1972	Matrimonial Causes Act 1973 (c. 18).
First report on family property: a new approach (Law Com. No. 52).	June 6, 1973	Legislative proposal deferred until later reports.
Solemnisation of marriage in England and Wales (Law Com. No. 53).	May 9, 1973	No.
Criminal Law: forgery and counterfeit currency (Law Com. No. 55).	July 18, 1973	No.
Personal injury litigation—assessment of damages (Law Com. No. 56).	July 25, 1973	No.

APPENDIX F

Postscript

The Law Commission's Eighth Annual Report has now been published. The Report explains and justifies the decision to change direction and method with regard to the Law of Contract. The codification project has been suspended. Work has moved from the general to the particular—presumably to areas where the need for reform is felt to be most urgent. When this has been done the Law Commission intend to consider afresh the production of a contract code. This is clearly sensible and as an observer/participant in a small part of the work one can only ruefully reflect that it is a pity that the Law Commission took so long to see this.

Next, the Report marks the growing impact of membership of the EEC on English Law reform especially in the area of Commercial Law. It is interesting to see the creation of a small Steering Group on Private International Law backed up by working groups on Corporeal and Incorporeal Property and Obligations and working parties on Foreign Money Liabilities and Conflicts of Jurisdiction affecting children.

The Law Commission remains, however, vitally concerned "with those aspects of law reform which are of direct significance in the lives of ordinary people." To reconcile this concern with the legal burdens of EEC membership may be difficult in the future.

As indicated in the text there is the beginnings of a "meaningful relationship" between the Law Commission and the Social Scientists. At present, however, the relationship looks to some more like that of patron and courtesan than an intellectual partnership let alone lawful matrimony. At another of those august gatherings held at All Souls in September 1972 we are told that "the principal positive conclusion ... was that some improvement might be made in the use of social sciences *in the service* of law reform." (The italics are mine). We are not told what the principal negative conclusions were.

The recent use of the Law Commission to consider controversial House of Lords decisions may obviate the need for prospective overruling provided that the Law Commission reports reasonably quickly.

The decline of the close relationship between the two Law Commissions mentioned in the text may have been arrested to a certain extent by the necessity to co-operate on EEC and other Private International Law matters and by a recent well meaning jamboree held North of the Border under the auspices of the profession.

As regards staffing one gets the impression that there are now more departmental representatives on committees and working parties and fewer academics and practitioners. If this is the case it is to be regretted. One of the great strengths of the Law Commission hitherto has been that it was to a large extent outside Government.

Another matter worth noting is that Professor Gower delivered a characteristically perceptive lecture entitled "Reflections on Law Reform" at the University of Toronto which is published in the Summer 1973 issue of the *University of Toronto Law Journal*, p. 257. His discussion of values in law reform activities in terms of "a vague utilitarianism, asking ourselves (subconsciously rather than consciously) what would conduce to the greatest good of the greatest number" (p. 268) is particularly interesting as is his residual "hankering after something more elegant based on premises more capable of articulation" (p. 269).

INDEX